HALF GODS

Akil Kumarasamy

HarperCollins *Publishers* India

First published in the US in 2018 by
Farrar, Straus and Giroux

This edition published in India by
HarperCollins *Publishers* in 2018
A-75, Sector 57, Noida, Uttar Pradesh 201301, India
www.harpercollins.co.in

2 4 6 8 10 9 7 5 3 1

P-ISBN: 978-93-5302-347-8
E-ISBN: 978-93-5302-348-5

Grateful acknowledgment is made to the following publications, in which some of these stories originally appeared, in slightly different form: *American Short Fiction* ("The Butcher"), *Boston Review* ("At the Birthplace of Sound"), *Glimmer Train* ("Brown Smurf"), *Guernica* ("Shade"), *Harper's Magazine* ("New World"), and *Massachusetts Review* ("A Story of Happiness," as "Meditations").

Designed by Richard Oriolo

Printed and bound at
Thomson Press (India) Ltd

This book is produced from independently certified FSC® paper to ensure responsible forest management.

For Appa

Man or god or demon, let him in!

—Mahabharata
(translated and retold by William Buck)

CONTENTS

HALF GODS

LAST PRAYER

RASHEED, MY OLD FRIEND, is a beauty with gray, sage-tinted fur and a lean, slick body that can fit under the crack beneath the sofa or into the cave of a dress shoe. With nine lives just like his namesake, he's the seer of ghosts, the killer of rodents, the warder of hopelessness. When I think of my friend, I cannot help but picture my brother: his face turned up to the sky, his mouth open, hands grasping the air.

The year before my grandfather died, the civil war in Sri Lanka ended and my brother had started praying. At night

Karna sat cross-legged under the maple tree in the backyard, hidden beneath the wilderness of Jersey. In the dark the tree and my brother looked like one tall shadow, and if not for the dim back porch light, they would have both blended perfectly into the evening sky. Summer fireflies flickered around him briefly like eyelids opening and then closing.

After school he sat chanting "Om Nama Sivaya" for hours at a time, waiting to be granted a boon. There was no stopping him. I would drag him from the yard by his armpits, my hands stinking with his sweat, but the moment he was loose, he ran back to the tree, barefoot, not breaking his chant. The afternoon our grandfather retold us the story of Kannagi and the King of Madurai, a tale of injustice, Karna was stung by a hornet on the soft, fleshy sole of his foot, but he swallowed his pain until our grandfather finished, and his foot had swollen into a luminous red ball he could not walk on for days.

We were like a family under house arrest, longing for privacy and fearful of solitude. When my grandfather locked himself in the bathroom for five hours, trying to drown out my mother's voice as she stood at the doorway with enough venom and grief to kill a small elephant, I asked my brother to at least pray for our peace of mind, but he shrugged me off with a reticence that was deeper than adolescence. I would speak to him and he would look right through me. I was eighteen that summer and only knew Sri Lanka through seasons of cease-fires and fighting, and I felt suddenly dumb and selfish then, asking for peace for myself.

At night when I closed my eyes, sleep never came easy. Nothing in dreams is safe. In bed during those vulnerable hours of night I caught stray transmissions from satellites that drifted in the heavens, the only true outside witnesses to the end of the war. As government forces shelled no-fire zones, aiming at hospitals, at Tamil civilians and rebels, naked bodies piled high for satellites that blinked and caught smudges.

On television all we saw of the end was celebration. Parades of men and women marched down the streets of the capital with banners and flags. They smiled and cheered at us as we mourned privately. My mother stood in vigil near the telephone, her eyes red and veiny and her nightgown wrinkled with sleep, while my grandfather watched television all day, trying to catch any news about the war, with the volume so high that I was sure he had lost all his hearing. I still needed to get through the school year and the months before I left for university. By then I was used to my body kicking into dormancy, the long stretch of waiting for life to begin. When my mother kept the gas on after boiling water for tea, no one bothered to turn it off until the stink burned our eyes. Later two of the bulbs went out in the family room and we sat around in darkness, disappearing except for the glare of the television.

We rationed through our days. We didn't wash our clothes or shower longer than three minutes. We ate pizza until we were all sick off the smell of grease and cheese. We shared a good night's rest between us, as if someone needed to be on guard, as if we were the survivors.

In the evenings, I ate my dinner outside alone and smoked whatever Rasheed left me. Those nights were mostly starless, so I would light up and make my own mini plasma ball that burned out in a few minutes. What else can you really do? I could still hear the wash of chatter from the television and recalled the tsunami from years ago, when my brother and I sat in our bathtub and held our breath, my mouth opening too soon as Karna whispered to me, "You're dead."

In the middle of a nightly broadcast, President Rajapaksa appeared on the screen in a white shirt and a noose of red cloth around his neck. His mustache grinned as he announced in Sinhala that there were no casualties from the war and the people of Sri Lanka were finally free from terror. On hearing his voice, my grandfather threw the mahogany-framed table clock against the wall.

The glass dome of the clock broke into shards and revealed the silver ticking. As I leaned over to pick it up, I rotated a finger along the sharp, circular motion, and held the hands tightly to make them stop. My cut was thin as a splinter. I looked up at this version of my grandfather who could no longer walk up the stairs or speak more than a sentence without feeling parched and tired but still managed to bash the house. I knew he had no plans on dying quietly. After one of his coughing fits, I had found him lying still on the sofa, his head turned inward, and just when I got close enough, an eyelash distance, he sprung at me, flexing his arms, calling my name like his favorite enemy.

He had grown up on a tea estate in Sri Lanka but spent years in the capital right when the war broke out. While other young men stayed and joined the rebels, my grandfather left the country. Brimmed with despair, he might have been a capable fighter, but since he chose the less heroic path, he made sure to find extra ways to suffer: worked the winter months outside without gloves or a proper jacket, drove a fifteen-year-old pickup truck with no AC, ruined one lung and didn't care to salvage the other.

He stared at the clock, which he had set nine and a half hours ahead so he would be on schedule with Sri Lanka. From the pantry, he handed me a shovel. "Make something fruitful of our misery," he said and then went to the kitchen to warm two bread slices between his palms.

I stood in the backyard and dug a zigzag of shallow wells into the earth. Handfuls of tulip seeds mixed with onion and bean blossoms. In the end, the garden looked more like a series of mousetraps. I fell asleep outdoors, sore and bruised, and in the early morning darkness woke to the sound of birds. Black feathers sprouted from each ditch. Beaks, the color of golden wheat, rattled with seeds.

All my efforts from the previous night ruined, I washed my hands and face with water from the hose and entered the house, which seemed more desolate. The walls painted a bleached yellow, grainy as pollen, and the hallway adorned with cheap photos of cats walking in gardens and impressive ships sailing on unnamed seas, all bought by my grandfather at yard sales, fishing through the ocean of his neighbors' garbage to find something usable rather than beautiful. Scattered around the rooms were knickknacks my grandfather had collected from places he had never visited—a bobblehead of the Mona Lisa, a Mickey Mouse lantern, a Stonehenge pepper shaker—and then my mother's subscription to *National Geographic*, the magazines piled high in our living room acting as a weight, a record of our thirteen-year stay. As a child, I dreamt of the house sinking into the wetland, falling and falling to the center of the earth. Other days I pictured tornadoes drifting from the Midwest and twirling in the backyard, undressing the house: first the gray shingles on the roof and then the plank sidings, leaving the house naked with its uncovered piping and fat chunks of insulation foam that would in time become a refuge for all the creatures of the Jersey forest. A beaver would chew the wooden frame of my bed as I slept.

AT THE END of June, Rasheed came home from university. Across the street in his room he offered me a blunt, and I felt content under that haze of smoke. I hadn't seen Rasheed since Christmas break. In that time he had lost his right molar and three hundred twenty dollars during a drunken New Year's Eve in Atlantic City but won seventy-five dollars the next month. According to my mother, he was a natural loser, but he was my first friend in the neighborhood and even my mother knew that was worth something.

Rasheed had completed his sophomore year but had failed three out of his five classes and accumulated nine hundred dollars' worth of parking tickets, and at the end of the semester, his father had taken his car keys and threatened him, holding out the electricity bill like a knife, saying that he needed to get his act together or else he would send him back to Bihar. As events turned out, it was his parents who returned to Bihar that summer for three weeks after Rasheed's uncle passed away.

While his parents were gone, we had the house to ourselves except for Rasheed's sister, Aisha, who was doing her residency in a hospital in Newark, and came home only to close her eyes for a few hours at night. In the mornings, Aisha spared her energy to say a few words to us or to the house that we were slowly making our own with unwashed dishes, bottles of liquor, and the flowery scent of weed and Febreze, and I would hear her voice roaming through each room and rousing me from the couch where I slept some days: "You bums," "Wretched boys," "Poor, poor Abba." She never told me to go home, but I could tell she wanted to. "Arjun, isn't your mother worried? Shouldn't you be taking care of your grandfather?" she'd say, and I would think of everything I knew and felt but couldn't show. "The two of you," she said, shaking her head, dismissing both of us. Long ago Rasheed had informed her how I never blinked in her presence, like I was afraid of losing her even for a second. Seven years older, she still teased me because I was scrawny, all chicken wire and hot air, but certain mornings I woke sweating beneath a blanket, and later in passing, she touched my forehead as if to check for a fever while I tried to fight the warmth rising in my face.

The house felt like an abandoned castle we had returned to. We were not kings but named if not for royalty then for greatness. I was the mythic prince Arjuna, and Rasheed was named after the wealthiest man in his father's village, who owned a few acres and his own livestock, which Rasheed said showed his father's expectations for him, but I always remembered what Rasheed's father said the evening Rasheed walked out of dinner after an argument about the state of his future. Sitting next to me, his father put down his fork and didn't move. He looked over the room, rested his eyes on the Quran. "I named you to be wise, a thinker, son," he said, though Rasheed couldn't hear him and wouldn't believe me even if I told him. For months, his father had refused to say his name and only referred to him obliquely by his sins. *The one who smells of liquor. The one who gambles. The one who breaks his mother's heart.* At the table, with Rasheed gone, his father paused on the word *son* and turned to me, touched my shoulder, and I knew he was speaking to me too.

Alone in the house, Rasheed and I waited for life to reveal itself. We would climb onto the roof after the sky had darkened. We could hear birds but not see them, and we called out to the unseen, the world around us.

MY GRANDFATHER WAS becoming more quarrelsome and one morning cornered me in the bathroom asking why I had clogged the sink. I said he was losing his mind like my mother, which he didn't like so I avoided him and didn't speak to him the rest of the day. It was only my brother, adrift in his own prayers, who called to me so clearly at night in the room that we shared. "Arjun," he'd say, "soon I will be granted a boon." He wouldn't tell me what he was going to ask for, as if anything he'd want would come true. We spoke in the dark, in brief exchanges. We hid from each other, but in rare glimpses I saw his nature fully—the unrelenting blueness of the sky, the endless dark pit of a sunflower—but always the moment passed before I could raise my voice, utter a simple sound: *you.*

When Rasheed was around, my brother would tell us a bad joke—*What do you call a rooster with no voice? A limp cock*—and let me in on his laughter. The beginning of adolescence had made him shy of his body. He'd hunch and compact his long arms and his bristle of legs, trying his best to reverse all that tiresome growing. If he said anything amusing or clever, he wanted both to be seen and to vanish before our eyes.

He looks more like my mother, who supposedly looks like my grandfather's mother, who was known for her beauty in a small fishing village on the coast of Jaffna. That's where the story ends and begins because my grandfather was always unwilling to speak of his own life. We knew about the journalist who was killed on his motorbike by paramilitary forces on a Wednesday afternoon before drinking tea, the white van that kidnapped my mother's classmate on his way back from school, the neighbor who died from fear when shells dropped near his home. My grandfather concealed himself in his stories, which became more vivid the farther he traveled from his own memories. Only myth had any real pleasure left for him. *The rubies in a broken anklet were worthless when Kannagi could not save Kovalan.*

Besides Rasheed I didn't know a single young person who called my grandfather by his whole name. "Mr. Muthulingham Padmanathan," he'd say, and wait for my grandfather to lift himself from his chair as he held the ridge of the cushion for balance, standing so still as not to reveal his limp. It was Rasheed's formality my grandfather appreciated, perhaps because he still longed for the ability to provoke a spark of fright in us, enough to keep our posture straight, he'd say. His scalp was dry with a ring of dark sunspots and his hands often seized with arthritis.

Some nights as I slept upstairs, my brother stayed with my grandfather in the study room my mother had converted into a bedroom. She had kept a few items, like the globe and the hardcover encyclopedias, fixtures from our school days, to remind us that things were not always this way. I rarely went into that room, especially when my grandfather became really sick, but at night, through my window, I thought I could hear them, their voices searching for me among the bushes and tiger lilies. Of course no one waited and called for me from below, and only that beguiling feeling of longing kept me up listening, so in the morning my sudden waking from a hard punch along my ribs left me restless, not ready for Rasheed's arrival, his desperate need to talk. He would go on about anything he heard or thought, and said things to me that he told no one else, probably because with me he had nothing to lose.

One afternoon he carried an issue of my mother's *National Geographic* magazines upstairs and started to read out loud an article about cobras. He never said it, but I knew he prided himself on his elocution, how he captivated people simply by opening his mouth. The truth was he didn't even need to open his mouth to persuade anybody. He was handsome and had girls asking him to jump fences to see them in their bedrooms, and in one year, he was seeing three chicks, all living within a quarter-mile radius of his house. He had a sharp memory and remembered things I wished he would forget. Like how I'd wanted to become a biologist to uncover the secret of life, the key to immortality, and Rasheed had showed me a handful of his jizz, curdling and creamy in the sunlight, and said everything I needed to know was right there, just waiting to be released.

After he closed the magazine and described how snakes used their cloaca for excretion and sex, he asked me if my grandfather ever joined the Tigers.

"His parents owned a store by a tea estate in Nuwara Eliya," I said. "Can you picture him fighting in the forest against the Sri Lankan army?"

"If someone killed my family, I would. Bomb an artillery ship, find some venomous snakes to unleash on their asses."

I thought of the army with their trophy shine and then the Tigers in the jungle, either extinct or endangered, using kerosene and sesame oil as fuel. My grandfather and his friends referred to the rebels casually as our boys, though there were girls too, while my mother cursed the Tigers for dying and not protecting the Tamil civilians in the end, leaving with all those early promises unfinished. After one of my mother's nightly phone calls, she reported to us that she now personally knew more of the dead than the living in Sri Lanka. My grandfather reached over to embrace her but she was squirming, her arms kicking like some injured gazelle, but he didn't let her go, and they both looked exhausted from keeping each other going. My grandfather lowered his voice and spoke to us patiently, forcing us to stretch out our necks.

"Tamil Eelam was never meant for people now, but for the future," he said.

He kept quiet and I couldn't hear any hope in what my grandfather said, but I was listening for it.

RASHEED SAID I come from a lineage of fighters because my father is a Punjabi Sikh and my mother is Eelam Tamil, but I didn't think so. My father's father wore a turban and carried a dagger, but my father is slim with short curly hair like me. He used to work long hours in finance and would carry a pocketknife, which he used to slice pears at his desk. Since my mother and grandfather resorted only to verbal violence, nothing from my known ancestry helped me when Rasheed placed me into a headlock and, practicing his wrestling moves, pummeled me with the back of his hand so there was no bruising, no evidence of pain. I was no match for Rasheed, who at the age of fourteen had fought a senior named Roland, who had his hair gelled into spears and wore sleeveless shirts. Rasheed left his mark before having his right hand crushed. He had known early on that our town in Jersey was not for him, and he had been fighting his way out of it since then.

I had plans to leave too. I was headed up north to Vermont in the fall. All I knew for certain was it would be colder than home, that I would need to build up layers of fat to survive. When I visited in the winter, I found that some people didn't even keep a fridge; they left all their groceries on the porch. Cracked frozen eggs preserved their shape.

Passing those houses, I felt a hunger I didn't realize I possessed. Rasheed, who ran the mile in a little over four minutes—the track team called him "Zero Gravity"—returned home his freshman year with a visible gut. "Beer," he told me as he jiggled his belly, but with his hairy face and snarl, I had heard *Bear*. Later, traveling through Vermont, I envisioned myself foraging outside strangers' houses, storing food supplies for the long hibernation, where I would sleep undisturbed with a roommate who wasn't my brother, hundreds of miles away from any place that resembled anything I knew.

My mother was not ready for me to leave because she could not handle more loss, even this temporary abandonment. She complained I spent too much time at Rasheed's place, and in response I stayed longer with Rasheed and returned only days later when I could not have known if she had wept or called out my name to induce more tears.

The evening my mother cooked her first real meal in weeks, Rasheed stayed for dinner. With my mother, he was always exceptionally polite, complimenting her culinary skills, which most nights consisted of tearing open a box of pasta and boiling water. He might have appeared smug if not for his curiosity. My grandfather spent a week teaching him chess, and Rasheed, only twelve then, didn't seem to mind losing to an old man, who roared at the board with his reedy battle cry every time he reached checkmate. Even then, Rasheed had a way of listening with his neck bent, eyes lifted like he could see underneath your words and find your true meaning. I suppose the silence of beautiful people contains the power to make you feel perfectly understood, though my mother didn't fall for his charm. Like Aisha, she didn't approve of Rasheed's behavior and considered his influence over me the sole reason for my own rebellious desires, but she treated him as a guest and was eager to ask him questions and for him to own and mend his flaws.

"How are you doing in school?" she said.

"Very well," Rasheed said, and my mother looked disappointed because she had known otherwise.

Rasheed sat next to Karna, and unwilling to reach over for more food, he ate from my brother's plate, a handful of fried rice, and with the loss, my brother's grin widened foolishly, full and satisfied.

"I don't see Aisha much," my mother said, "she must be busy in the hospital."

"People are always getting sick," Rasheed said.

As if on command, my grandfather started choking on a piece of chicken he had not chewed properly, and my mother shot up, looking frantically for water, and I ran to him with my half cup and tried to make him swallow.

"Bend him forward," Rasheed said, and after a slap my grandfather continued eating like nothing had happened. He asked for more chicken, and my mother quietly thanked Ganesh, Shiva, Muruga, any god she could think of except us.

I didn't hang out with Rasheed for almost a week after that evening. From my room, I sometimes saw him sitting on the roof, talking on the phone or smoking. If I left he was gone by the time I returned, and I had the vague feeling that I hadn't seen him at all. He had friends who swung by and picked him up for parties. Now and then during the day, when Aisha was away at work, a girl showed up at the door ringing the bell.

Though we hadn't spoken in days, I wasn't surprised when he came over in the afternoon with a black eye. He winked at me from the doorway, and I saw the color spread across his eyelid in the darkening shade of a sunset. We drank upstairs in my room from the whiskey I stored under the bed. Lying on the sheets, Karna traced the outline of an old Batman sticker on the ceiling. In the fourth grade, he gave a nine-word monologue in the voice of the superhero: *I am mysterious, a human hiding inside a bat.*

Rasheed leaned against the window and we could hear barbecues, children's laughter caught in the scent of smoke and burgers. "Aisha kicked me out for the day," he said. "She doesn't want her fiancé to see the mess, or maybe just me."

"Aisha has a fiancé," I repeated.

"He's a real asshole," Rasheed said and balanced his arm on my shoulders like he wanted to tell me I was the better choice.

I didn't ask him about the black eye, maybe because I was so used to seeing Rasheed falling apart, but really I was thinking of myself and feeling what might have been jealousy under different circumstances, if I thought Aisha might one day have interest in me. In my selfishness, I had wished her a life of loneliness, in eternal service of her patients rather than in the arms of someone else.

By the time evening rolled over us, we were faded and couldn't move even if we'd been dragged and set on fire. Rasheed spoke without troubling his lips, and my brother, who had downed four shots of whiskey, returned from the kitchen holding a whole chocolate cake, incriminating in his indulgence. He stood at the doorway, drowsy, and when he turned to Rasheed, it took all my energy to grab the cake from his hands and frown at his eagerness. He should have been in the yard chanting like some half-naked yogi, and when I reminded him, he looked at me with such hatred and shame. I turned away because that was what I wanted to see.

Only after my mother and grandfather slept did we stumble to the backyard, tripping over my mother's potted plants and stone designs. Rasheed showed us the tooth he was missing, and Karna poked his finger through the open window of his mouth. Rasheed said he thought it made him look dignified, like a breast pocket on a suit. We were lying around in the grass and staring up at the sky, and if someone had passed us then, in our quiet, they might have mistaken us for dead.

"I would rather sleep out here from now on," Rasheed said. He wanted to drive all the way west to Yellowstone and live among all the wildlife, which had been my dream too at some point.

Out of spitefulness or kindness, maybe both, I told Rasheed to take Karna. I knew my brother would want to join him. "He spends a quarter of his day under a tree," I said. "He's perfect. Just make sure he brings his inhaler."

Rasheed turned toward my brother. "What do you say, Karna?"

I was having difficulty focusing. My head hurt and I felt so warm that I wanted to dig myself into the cool earth as I had seen my neighbor Mr. Wu do with his tulip bulbs. As I contemplated the best way to stand upside down, certain the cold would beat the blood rush, Rasheed decided we should drive to the creek by our old middle school and try to fish with my grandfather's rod. I didn't think there were any fish in the stream, but Rasheed insisted, smiling with all his remaining teeth.

Below the footbridge, there were only patches of water, and in the summer heat the mud had mostly dried into firm ground, but still Rasheed swung the rod. He didn't have good aim and kept landing the hook in the branches of tall, leafy trees. Stars reflected underneath us, and I remembered a Tamil word for them, sky fish, and I wanted to tell Rasheed to cast his line into the sky, but he was too busy whipping and yelling at the foliage.

My brother looked over the wooden railing and that fatalistic edge I'd always known in him surfaced, glinting under the moonlight.

"I caught a big one," Rasheed said and grimaced through his elbow, pulling back until he snapped the hook.

I swatted at mosquitoes circling my head. "Enough," I said, but they multiplied, growing stronger despite my words and attacking everything, finding their way under the skin.

On the way back, I ran over a cat, a lump along the road I first mistook for nothing more than a blur of trash. There had been no sound, no murmur of pain. "Poor thing," Rasheed said, and I wanted to kill him right there too as I drove in my grandfather's old pickup truck, raging with my grandfather's temper, my trifle inheritance. I pulled the truck over and vomited on the curbside under the streetlamp, hours before dawn.

MY FATHER VISITED us when he had a conference in Jersey. The last time I had seen him was for my high school graduation. He had handed me an empty shoebox wrapped in gold paper that held within it three crisp hundred-dollar bills. My mother called the gift generous, but looking at the box, I had expected more.

He now sat in the living room eating biscuits as my mother held the wallet-sized photo of his newly born daughter. She was half-Japanese, but I couldn't tell. I sat across from him while Karna greeted him and then went off to pray in the backyard, where Rasheed was discreetly smoking.

My father was always pleasant and understanding with me, so I couldn't stand him. Shaking hands, he'd look closely at my face and seem to want to feel not bone and muscle but the essence of my thoughts. In our limited time, I couldn't give him any more than *yes*es, *no*s, and a few strings of words that didn't add up to anything.

We almost had a real conversation a year and a half ago when my father took Karna and me to a park in Jersey City, where he used to hang out with my mom and his brother when they were kids. It was more a plot of grass with some trees and two benches, brightened with a collage of plastic wrappers and aluminum cans. My father had picked up a Corona like he was about to drink from it but then poured it out, let the liquid puddle next to our feet, murky as piss. "Your uncle would come out here in the middle of the night and sometimes fall asleep, and I'd find him stretched out on one of these benches in the morning like a bum," he said and paused. "Like he didn't even have a home."

I had wanted to ask my father if he missed my uncle, how sometimes I didn't believe he really existed. I was five the last time I had seen him and the world felt then like a flat horizon that would go on and on, my mother and father together, the three of us living in our own house on that wiry road leading to nowhere, the back hills of Kentucky where old racing horses wandered and ate rotten apples.

My mother kept no photographs of her time in Kentucky or her teenage years in Jersey, and sometimes I had difficulty placing her anywhere except in relation to me. Like we were born together. When I mentioned my uncle's name late one night, my mother shooshed me with the tips of her fingers and before I could even notice a tremble of recognition, she looked behind her as if she heard someone steal away into the house. She went to find my brother, who was asleep on the couch, and without waking him, she cradled his curled body, gave me his foot to hold like he was our lucky charm that would keep us safe.

My mother poured my father some coffee, and watching him stare at her, I wished she had looked more lovely, her face open and startling, a beginning rather than an end.

After my father left, my grandfather said I should treat him with more respect, which was unlike anything he had said of my father in the past. To him, I was always acting like my father, either too stubborn and unforgiving or not stubborn enough and too forgiving. My father became everything we were lacking. I told my grandfather he must be losing his mind to say anything partial about my father. Instead of reprimanding me, he laughed and for the first time in a while he sounded happy.

TWO DAYS BEFORE Rasheed's parents returned, he decided to throw a party. Aisha had night shifts at the hospital and wouldn't return home that weekend. It was a small get-together, mostly Rasheed's friends from college. On the night of the party, we arranged the bottles and shaved our faces, which we hadn't done in days. We had gotten looks from customers at the supermarket and shot back with strokes of our beards.

While we all drank, Karna sipped soda from a glass. A girl with pink streaks in her hair threw her cards on the table and rushed to the bathroom after the second round of Kings. Rasheed talked to a girl with a nose ring and zebra pants. He had his hand on her knee and smiled whenever she spoke. She drank careful sips, told him about the last poetry slam she'd performed at, and didn't look down at his hand, not once. Dressed in his formal clothes, a striped button-down and slacks, Karna watched the two of them. Rasheed twirled a strand of the girl's hair on his finger like a wedding band before he took her hand and they disappeared upstairs. I was flirting with a girl with toasted orange skin, who kept drinking screwdrivers, which in my mind made her skin more orange. My brother also disappeared the rest of the evening, and I found him hours later asleep in our room, quiet, even after I walked into our wardrobe and fell into his twin bed before finding my own.

AISHA SAID RASHEED fell off the roof, and maybe he did but I was never sure. She found him in the morning by the shed lying like some brilliant comet that had flashed across the sky and crumbled onto Earth.

At the hospital, Aisha sat beside him in a metal chair holding his wrist, his fingers loose and limp, not ready for a fight. If Rasheed were still conscious, he would have been amazed at how his bones broke, the way nothing in him broke clean, his own rib cage puncturing his lungs. We arrived in the early evening and Rasheed was speaking through machines and vents. My mother held Aisha, who wasn't crying but sat with her arms folded, hardening herself for what was to come. Their parents were flying across land and ocean, and in a matter of a day would hover over us, and for all Aisha dreaded, through that turbulence of air, they might see their son ascending toward them.

My grandfather was irritable and couldn't keep still so he spent the time admiring the hospital. He rarely visited my mother when she worked, but now he wandered the hallways and visited the rooms of strangers lying alone in slanted beds who must have been accustomed to the sight of passing strangers watching over them. The fluorescent overcast made patients look ugly, except for Rasheed, maybe because he was not awake to show fear.

In the hospital, death can smell so clean, prepackaged, bacteria-free. I think that's why my grandfather turned to my mother and said quietly, "Don't let me die in a place like this."

I thought of the safe zones, bodies piled in the open, uncremated, unburied, in Mullivaikkal. Enough dead to fill entire cities I have never visited.

Late at night when I'd listen to my mother crying over the phone, I'd sometimes touch my face and feel the shape, the architecture of bones, and then all at once I'd fall apart into the never-ending, my mother saying, "Useless. This life was for what?" Though I had believed we'd been cursed from the beginning, I'd always known, even before my grandfather called to me with the blunted edge of his voice from his deathbed, that we were the lucky ones.

My mother let Aisha sleep and said she'd watch Rasheed through the night. It was the first time my mother had cared for him. She combed his hair with her fingers and spoke to him like he could hear us.

When my grandfather brought us home, I could still hear her voice down the corridor, the tail end of a whisper.

We ate cereal for dinner. Together we finished a whole box of Mini-Wheats, and Karna almost swallowed the copper coin prize. No one could sleep, so we stayed up watching television, squeezed side by side, and I thought how one day I might miss sitting on the couch with the only family I knew. My grandfather kept tapping my head to give me any comfort he had left to offer, which wasn't much but wasn't nothing. In the middle of a commercial, he lowered the volume and began to tell a story, and I thought it would be about the war or ancient Tamil literature, but it was about us.

"I was thinking about when you two played manhunt with the neighborhood kids, and no one could find Karna. We were worried, thinking he was missing. But Arjun found him, knew where he would think to hide."

"He peed his pants waiting to be found," I said and turned to Karna, who had closed his eyes, his mouth parted for prayer.

We visited Rasheed in the hospital the next day and the next. Even after his parents arrived, we went or I went alone. Rasheed's mother stayed with him during the day, and his father read to him from the Quran at night after work. He finally had his son by his side, unable to go anywhere, but he wasn't sure if Rasheed could hear him. Still he read on until he tired, mostly for himself.

That summer before I left home, before my grandfather

died, I hardly slept, and I remember on the night of my brother's last prayer looking through the bedroom window and seeing him collapse into the dry grass by the porch light with his hands and legs shaped into a fox. Only after a minute did he sit up and begin to dig, searching the earth for its dark secret, and I wondered if, like my grandfather had instructed, he was going to make something of our misery.

Karna returned to bed and we did not speak for years. Even later when we began to rely on each other and we both had our share of heartbreaks, he still never revealed his boon, but I know he used it for Rasheed because he did live. He lived countless times, through a car accident, a seven-story-building fire, an upturned boat on the bend of the Colorado River, a grueling horse ride in a sun-drenched desert, a divorce that left him hitchhiking alone across the country. He lived.

NEW WORLD

ON THE EVE OF INDEPENDENCE, Sir William drove away from the estate in his cream-colored Morris and left his fortunes in the hands of Mr. Balakumar, the Tamil manager, who promptly brought his milch cows to Sir William's private garden to feed on the roses. We had the day off, but still we woke early and stood at the edge of the tea field, watching through the morning fog. For days, weeks, when we tried to remember Sir William's face, his light blue eyes, we could picture only his car winding down the hillside of Nuwara Eliya and vanishing like a cloud.

Above the tea fields, rows of houses stretched across the horizon like a string of baby teeth, small and overcrowded. Our grandparents had lived in these houses, one-room caves with tin roofs, and if they were alive, they would still recognize their homes, everything as they left it, only the coat of whitewash brighter. They didn't own these houses, and our inheritance was what they could fit inside: a wooden chair, a teakettle, maybe a chessboard. "We live as we die, owning nothing," our parents had been told, and they reminded us of it each day until even our own shit was more of an offering than a possession.

Our grandparents had crossed the waters between India and Ceylon, and our parents spoke to us about death simply as both a certainty and a choice. Either stay and die of hunger, drown in the dark waters, or languish in an unknown land. Following each possibility to the end, we let ourselves turn into dried carcasses, our hair shed, blood soured, and then in the open sea, bodies bloated into plump blue women, until we reached the final death up here in the pungent, cool hillside that still awaited us.

Standing idle in the field, we pictured Sir William sailing off from our warm island to a colder one, men and women with buttery faces greeting him on his arrival. Unrecognizable perhaps after all these years, crushing cardamom and ginger in his tea, rinsing his mouth with sesame oil for salubrity, he'd return home and wake to the smell of wet wood and lichen, pink-scaled fish with horns for breakfast, giant eels sliding through the sky on his morning stroll as he searched for the hillside, the wisp of paradise. All week, a voice on the radio assured us everything would be reborn in the coming day. Even the trees would look different, because they would be *our* trees. Each breath you took would be *your* breath. As if all these years, we had been borrowing our lives.

We collected newspapers with pictures of the new prime minister. He was broad-shouldered and wore trousers, dress shirts, and jackets in the fashion of Sir William and Mr. Balakumar. When he first spoke on the radio, he talked in English and we didn't understand a word of what he said. Then he switched to Sinhala, and we still didn't understand. We only caught the word *Ceylon* and it felt foreign, faraway. Another country.

For the celebration, the men cooked goat, a gift from Mr. Balakumar, and the children danced around the slaughtering as we rested for once in the field, surrounded by freshly picked bushes. Under a gray sky fattening with rain clouds, we unfolded our arms and legs, sank into the dry stretch of our bodies. We played color games, sang girlhood rhymes to distract us from our worries hiding in the bushes as everything and nothing changed.

When we heard Selvakumar, we instinctively smiled and thought of early mornings between dreams and waking when we could simply linger, empty-handed, in the sound of an owl or fox. He wore an oversized yellow shirt, and had not grown more than a fingernail in the past two years, and we didn't know if he ever would. We believed Selvakumar would always look this way: a child, who salvaged odd, broken things such as a bronze figurine of a horse missing a leg, an ivory comb with gap teeth, a sparrow with one wing. As he worked alongside us picking tea leaves, performing ladies' work in place of his sick mother, we let him into our jokes, showed the calluses scarring our feet, and told him about the bleeding that left us lightheaded and slow. He was twelve, but we treated him as if he were older, a long-lost son who had returned to us. There was a story of a young man who ejaculated into a river and whose seed was swallowed by a fish, which became a human baby. Sometimes we imagined Selvakumar was that boy, still smelling of river water and damp mud. He had grown, it seemed, outside our wombs.

On rainy days when the chill kept us cursing, we shortened Selvakumar's name into a girl's, Selvi, and he would stick out his tongue at us, call us madwomen, which warmed our spirits. We were his nuisance, his heartache, all the mothers he never truly had. The month before, Mr. Balakumar had beaten the boy for ruining a bush with his carelessness. "The bud and two leaves, not too old, not too young," he repeated as he whipped him with sugarcane, until all the sweetness left Selvakumar smelling of burnt molasses, his skin the sticky color of a beet. Throughout the night, we sat by his side, held his hand, and took turns tending to him. He didn't sleep, just stayed quiet, staring at the gold-filled tooth he had found by Sir William's house with Vani on her birthday. She was twenty-eight that day, and when he gave it to her as a present, she asked him what was more precious, the metal or the human matter. Three weeks later she died on a sunny afternoon from exhaustion. Talkative and twig-limbed, she looked peaceful lying down, finally getting some proper rest.

"What's wrong, Mr. Prime Minister?" we asked.

Selvakumar didn't look at us. "How can an Indian bastard be prime minister?"

"You shouldn't listen to Muthu. He's only repeating something his father said."

Their friendship was uneven, Selvakumar two years older than Muthu but a whole head shorter. Muthu's father, Mr. Padmanathan, ran the estate store and considered himself a big boss, though Sir William bought a controlling share of his property years ago. Even Mr. Balakumar was one of the boy's distant relatives. Sooner or later we knew the boys would grow into their families.

Lying in the field, Selvakumar waved his right hand at the sky and we followed the chalklike trace of his fingertips. "Water," he said. "All made of water."

Muthu had been teaching Selvakumar from the lessons he learned at school. Mr. Padmanathan disapproved of this practice, but still didn't prohibit the giving of scraps, a handful of bare-bone English sentences.

Everything Selvakumar learned, we heard too. While picking leaves, he recited to us random bits of natural history, and we were lost in the quickness of his tongue. On the morning we discovered the sudden bloom of grasshoppers, Selvakumar told us about the explorer named Marco Polo, who traveled to China and along the Malabar Coast of India, where he first saw women smeared with oil standing outside under the high noon sun darkening their skin for beauty.

"This Marco Polo must be mad," we told him. "Only laborers stand in the sun."

"Everything was different then," he said.

"You mustn't listen to Muthu. Who knows if this Marco Polo even lived?"

But really we were warning him against his own heart, already drifting kilometers and kilometers away from the hillside.

MR. PADMANATHAN'S STORE once served tourists interested in buying miniature models of hill station trains made out of dark chocolate and finely engraved sandalwood boxes for tea leaves, but his business did poorly, and by the third year, he began to sell belongings from his home, recycling his wife's saris into patterned placemats and the rugs into blankets, leaving the house bare, stripped of its comforts, with only four chairs as furniture. Sir William insisted on purchasing a share of the shop after the original estate store became infested with rats and burned down. Mr. Padmanathan couldn't afford to protest. He put away his porcelain teakettles and saffron-dyed lace and began to sell plain, everyday items.

To save money, he diluted the arrack but sold the drink at full price to our husbands. We didn't mind, because he saved us from some trouble. Still, we didn't trust him. He was Tamil too, but we didn't call him brother, and after we paid, he whispered about us, called us Indian coolies. None of us had ever visited India, but he didn't care about those details. Like Mr. Balakumar, he prided himself on his ancestry and spoke of lineage most adamantly around his son.

Remember you're Ceylon Tamil, he'd say, your great-great-great-great-grandfather was the king's adviser.

Selvakumar first noticed Muthu two years ago. Muthu was sitting outside the store wearing a Jesuit school uniform, his spindly calves covered by red wool socks. Something about the socks and the way the boy mumbled to himself made Selvakumar pause, long enough for Muthu to ask if he could whistle.

"The crow over there with the hungry eyes is my grandfather," Muthu said.

Later he would tell us how they sat and ate biscuits in the darkness of the store's pantry, where onions and potatoes were stored. He brought us back a packet and instructed us to eat with closed eyes as we sensed the pleasure of a sweet and satisfying blindness.

When we watched the pair run around the hillside, slapping lizards with twigs, we privately warned Selvakumar. "Be careful of him."

"There, there, Amma Kuti," he would say, and pat us on the

cheek like we were children that needed to be soothed. Then he boiled us a brew of tea dust as he did for his mother.

IN THE DULL glare of the afternoon, Mr. Balakumar inspected the charring goat and pronounced the men, women, and children as lucky witnesses to the independence of their nation. He touched the belly of an expectant mother and said her baby would be born free and know nothing of white men from a cold island. "Here, here!" he yelled, holding out a bottle of arrack before taking a swig. "We rejoice in the new day for us, for Ceylon."

He took another swig, drinking with the occupational vigor of Sir William, who was once a soldier in India, though the only combat he endured was drinking gin and quinine in the fight against malaria. We all remembered Mr. Balakumar weeping as Sir William drove away, but we could not tell if it was from sadness or joy as he hugged the blue lapels of the suit jacket Sir William left for him.

Mr. Balakumar was a heavy man with the strategic, stern face of a clerk. His wife stood quietly behind him, clutching their two-year-old son. She looked suspiciously at us, wondered if we had received gifts from her husband, if he had taken any special interest in one of us. Her gaze came to rest on Selvakumar's mother, who sat in a gray sari by the cast-iron pot of boiled rice as a rooster with striking red plumage strutted toward her; the contrast between her and the bird left her looking drained of color, weak. The skin on her arms and neck was speckled with pale dots, and clumps of her hair were missing, revealing slivers of scalp. She once had been attractive, and we were both envious and grateful then not to have the burden of it. Four years ago, she had a child as pale as Sir William's Morris, and before it could become her shame and salvation, it died, only a week old.

We joined her by the cast-iron pot and sang harvest songs, knowing nothing else to sing for the occasion. Lakshmi had cut out pictures of the prime minister from newspapers and we agreed he looked handsome but prideful.

Our husbands, meanwhile, drank with Mr. Balakumar. We had never seen him acting so freely with them. He slapped their shoulders and they exchanged bottles, kissed the rims still wet with each other's saliva. If he weren't wearing his suit, they might have been equals, breathing and enjoying the same air. Suddenly our husbands' hopes for their own crops and livestock felt possible. Maybe they would have three Mahalakshmi cows and enough lentils for a year. The estate might stop growing tea.

Selvakumar sat next to his mother with the tail of her sari wrapped around him. Bundled together, they leaned on each other, heads delicately balanced. He asked if she was thirsty as he took her hand. He took his mother's hand and didn't budge even when Muthu appeared at the gathering.

Everyone greeted the boy politely, knowing his father from the estate store and his relation to Mr. Balakumar. Propriety kept Muthu's hands in his pockets.

"Do you know the prime minister says he has a third eye?" he said. "He can tell the future. He'll know what will happen in the country. That's what he says."

He glanced toward Selvakumar. His belief that Selvakumar was his closest friend was something he did not question. We too remembered what it had been like to be girls, to make promises that could never be kept.

Muthu left two bananas near his friend's feet. "Om Guru Selvakumar," Muthu began, his hands folded in prayer. "Please bless these bananas as an offering for the new country."

He bowed and Selvakumar couldn't help but laugh as he touched the head of his sole devotee. Without a word, they ran into the evening and looped around the houses as if nothing had changed.

Mr. Balakumar stood before the feast and raised another bottle. "In India, they received their independence and acted like animals. Hindus killing Muslims, Muslims killing Hindus. We will be different, more civilized."

We ate quickly. When was the last time we had eaten meat? Two months ago, perhaps. Who could afford it? Someone had decorated Mr. Balakumar's cows with garlands and turmeric. Kuppuswami played the nadaswaram poorly, but once we were too full to move, he performed a wedding rhythm, and the young ones in the group danced. We all clapped our hands, counting the beats, the minutes until the new day arrived.

Over the hillside the sun broke into a golden yolk before drifting below the mountains. Muthu and Selvakumar held out their banana peels at the edge of the cliff across from the feast.

"To Ceylon!" they yelled and dropped the peels.

They twisted and writhed in the air, a pair of falling stars.

THE RAIN SMELLED of camphor and matchsticks. As the sky darkened, we could hear trembles of thunder in the distance. We opened our mouths to drink, and the water teased us, drop by drop. Our grandparents would tell us stories of those faraway towns of Madurai, Thirunelveli, Thiruchi, where the land was dry and people died of famine. We were afraid of places we could only imagine, and felt lucky to live on land so green.

Mr. Balakumar washed his face with the rain, splashed liquor around his mouth, let it trickle to his neck. We enjoyed him better this way, and we wondered if his true self had yet to be revealed. As the men tried to sober up, they decided to make a wager on Mr. Balakumar's cows. They pooled their money and he agreed on the game of his choosing: horseshoes. His wife groaned, but Mr. Balakumar insisted, and she reluctantly set up the stakes. Tending to a man as demanding and fat as Mr. Balakumar must be difficult. "Raychel," he said, and she looked over at him. "Bring me *my* set of horseshoes."

We knew her only as Mrs. Balakumar. Her Christian name felt oddly intimate, as if we had seen her in her nightgown, drinking a cup of tea, her hair loose.

The rain thickened; droplets interlaced momentarily into silver webbing. Paari was elected as the representative for the group. He was chosen for the lightness and precision of his hand, the way he could prune the skinniest branch without tarnishing the rest. Mr. Balakumar puffed out his chest and slapped the muscle under Paari's arms. "You sure you want this bony fellow?" he asked. "If I win, no pay for three days."

Paari agreed but we were all frowning. We would either go hungry or feast on yogurt and milk. We imagined our own children reaching their proper heights and secretly we wondered if we still had any growing left in us, if we were all just stunted giants.

Mr. Balakumar coiled back his wet hair, extended his arms, and took aim. He threw the horseshoe far but crooked.

When it was Paari's turn, the crowd chanted his name wildly, shouted out advice about his stance. The rain-slicked U flew high but stopped short of Mr. Balakumar's. It was best out of twenty, we reassured ourselves. In that curve of metal our hopes wavered, flew, and crashed to the earth. As we cheered for ourselves through Paari, any doubts we had were lost in the drama of our voices.

The two men took their time, while above them sound and light circled each other until they met in a spectacular shrill blaze. We were winning before the downpour began.

We swallowed mouthfuls, tasted a saltiness, and knew we must be wading through the sea. From our one-room shelters, we peeked through bare windows and felt both excitement and dread as the water blew inside and combed through our lives, so much more porous than we had believed. The dye in the paper calendar bled along the wall and the single encyclopedia crumbled into soggy fragments. Outside a sad doll floated by in a stream already jammed with baskets and shards of arrack bottles. Our winning cattle shrieked and slid through the mud. Our children huddled around us as the tin roof distorted into an insatiable belly. Our daughter yelled, "It's Ganesh!" We thought she was right, because only the Elephant God could turn wreckage into prosperity.

We stood by the doorway, unsure of where to risk our lives. In the end, we bet on the open skies rather than the damp walls of our small homes, already beginning to smell of black mold. As we assembled on the dirt road under the beating rain and watched our roofs collapse, we pictured our old selves dying, crushed by the weight of all our previous days. Whatever was left of our girlhood survived in modest things: the stones our daughters carried in their pockets, and the shriek of a koel bird we had dreamt of eating for its voice. For the new world, we must all transform, shed our skin and rename everything. The flowers were stripped, the trees slanted with torn limbs, and we needed to make sense of it while the water shriveled us into old women and plowed through the land to bring new life.

Our children clung to us tighter. We own none of this, we reminded them patiently, and their wide eyes looked over the imploded houses, the silver sheen of metal, as they pointed at their buried things.

We imagined bare tea bushes underwater, the buds floating and brewing in liquid, warm with humidity. When Mr. Balakumar returned to his senses, he would count each pillaged bush, calculating his losses because he loved to accrue misfortune. But for now, Mr. Balakumar lay senseless in a wagon, slumbering while his wife struggled to push him with her son tied to her back. She cursed him in a way she normally would never have dared. Coarse Pig, Fat Donkey, Stinky Radish Face. She seemed to enjoy herself, paused to rest under an awning with her husband's feet sticking out in the rain.

We felt almost tender toward him in his infantile state, but we knew better than to be fooled by a single day. He would make us work twice as hard to compensate for the holiday and destruction. "Pick doubly fast," he would say, and we would curse him as we concocted plans to reincarnate into Durga with eight arms so we could pick with four times the speed.

In a dream we sometimes had, the men didn't trim the bushes and we didn't pick. Ripe koruntus went unplucked. The bushes finally grew into trees with full pink blossoms, resurrecting the ancient forest that had existed long before our grandparents ever left their villages and crossed the sea. As the rain blinded us, we waited for that world, our feet buried in wet dirt, soft as a womb, our heads raised.

AFTER THE WEATHER quieted, we fell asleep by the ruins of our homes and woke to our independence. We were sick, feverish in our mops of clothing. Surrounded by strange marshland, we felt this aching thirst and greeted the sight of our new nation with delirium.

Together we assessed the damage. To varying degrees, the houses were dented, lopsided, fully collapsed. Because they formed a line connected side by side, the overall structure had the appearance of a flattened snake, unevenly crushed. The houses had been built in a matter of days, and we were certain they would rise up in less. Inevitably the damage was compared, and those who fared better gloated about an unhinged door still standing. Children's injuries were measured by the severity of pain. A twisted ankle was not as notable as a numb, blue arm.

Selvakumar's mother, bleached of all color, limped along the roadside and called out for her son. We tried to think of when we had last seen him, but all we could picture was his face from weeks ago, when he chewed betel nuts with Muthu, grinning at us with his cherry red teeth.

We searched through the field, and parted the bushes for the boy we prayed was still alive. We hoped he had not rushed ahead of her in fear of witnessing her death. "I'll be alone," he said the morning she hacked up blood, and we wiped his face as he closed his eyes, reached out to us in the dark.

A tattered pink sari clung to the branch of a tree and we paused in silence as if staring at a bright, defeated flag. Along the tea field, battles had been fought, the winners unknown. If Sir William returned, he would stand on the tallest hill and say, "My, my, they sure did make a mess of it."

Tea leaves dotted the earth in the shape of baby footprints. Young shrubs were upturned by their roots. The storm exposed what was concealed under the ground. Rich red soil, dense with iron, emerged in clumps the size of anthills, and children molded it like precious clay, straight from the center of the earth. Sparrows were more fearless after having lost their nests; they strutted beside us, claiming material to rebuild.

The sun spread over us, reflecting all the trapped water. By the time we discovered the yellow-tipped butterfly on the fat corpse, Muthu's father had rounded the hillside, towing his son by the ear with one hand and consoling the wailing Mrs. Balakumar with the other.

BEFORE ANY TALK of death, Mr. Padmanathan first dealt with the living, his son who didn't have the sense to know he was being robbed when he had handed over everything in the cashbox to his friend.

"We were going to Independence Day ceremonies in the capital," the boy repeated over and over again, unable to comprehend anything, his brain still sopping wet from the storm.

Love might have disarmed him of caution, but buried within it was raw dust, gunpowder. We could hear a trigger: *Indian coolie.*

Mr. Balakumar possessed an even smile, with his teeth peeking over his bottom lip as if he found death unremarkable, worthy of only three-teeth derision. On the curve of his neck was a puncture wound. He might have drowned in a puddle and been pierced by a sharp object. Or a bird might have pecked through his jugular. Or he decided to perform a last-minute sacrifice for the new nation. But all anyone could see was Selvakumar's absence and an empty cashbox. No sane person, they agreed, would choose to leave verdant hillside for the crowded filth of cities.

Mrs. Balakumar declared that if the boy returned, he would have equal punishment. She sliced the air near her throat, and Selvakumar's mother wept quietly, and we knew she wouldn't make it through the week without her son. We looked toward the bend of the hillside and waited for the methodical rattling of the old train, imagining the relief we would feel if we saw him, which would only show as anger. Alone in an unknown city, a child who collected injured things: How would he survive?

Mr. Padmanathan folded his son's ear into a throbbing knot. The boy's face broke apart like a teacup. "We will be compensated," Mr. Padmanathan promised, and he and Mrs. Balakumar talked of police and justice.

We felt Mr. Balakumar turning his wet, dead face toward us. *In India, they act like animals, killing each other.*

What would become of us? Secretly, we knew we would be the ones to pay, though we had done nothing wrong.

This was our new beginning, we chanted to ourselves as the pink sari flailed in the wind. From the shape of the fabric, we saw a shadow of a man made from no more than fallen branches and dark leaves. Just for a moment, we were possessed with the prime minister's power and we could see all our desires for Selvakumar's future. He is an actor in a film with M. G. Ramachandran, then he's a teacher, a doctor, a train conductor. He has a pretty, dainty-necked wife who simply lounges about, and three or four children running around, grabbing at his limbs as he tells them stories of the hillside where the women curse and laugh, standing under the beating sun and becoming more beautiful.

A STORY OF HAPPINESS

The baby was born with a tail like a monkey. He was a furry thing with black hair curling everywhere, even on the flap of his tongue. The father said the mother had eaten too much spinach or had made love to Lord Hanuman. The mother couldn't stand to look at the baby. She would take out a knife and stare at the baby in the reflection of the blade. The hairy monster giggled at her. The father said a child is a child, even an ugly child. He affectionately called

the boy his little baboon, but one night when they all slept in the same room, the mother carried the baby outside and under a streak of moonlight, she dug a hole in the dirt with a spoon and buried the baby, who kept smiling until the last spoonful. In three months, tall bushels of curry leaves would grow from the mound, tasting particularly bitter for the season.

AN OLD SINHALESE WOMAN HANDED me her prayer beads when I was on a train returning from my mother's funeral in the hills of Nuwara Eliya. I was twenty and working in Colombo and thought I had grown out of such childhood comforts as tears. Streaks of vibhooti lined my forehead from the temple, and the offering of her beads was unusual, but I accepted them, too run-down with grief to refuse. And when they sat in my hands like a sullen worm, she moved my thumb clockwise and spoke to me in quiet Sinhala and though I understood only pieces of her words, I knew she wanted me to pray. She covered my hands with such belief that it did not matter I was a Hindu bending over Buddhist beads. Nothing prepared us for death. I closed my eyes, chanted after Lord Shiva. Om Nama Sivaya. I fell into those words, and time slowed with my fingers. And when I awoke from that state, the woman was gone. She had left me with her prayers.

LAALINI, THE WOMAN I married, recited for me three lines of poetry about this world of dew and confessed her love for Issa, and before I learned he was a poet, I thought he was an old lover and the revelation left me walking the city in a trance as if I had almost lost what was irretrievable.

MY FRIEND VICTOR at work told me his wife was pregnant. In celebration, instead of mowing the field, we sat behind the baseball bleachers, away from the school, and drank warm beers Victor had wrapped in his shirt. It was early summer, and without the children, the school felt like a gravesite we tended, picking at soda cans and plastic bags, leveling the grass. Victor once found three used condoms by the swings and kicked the ground, cursing. Later he planted tulips at the spot.

Victor told me his fifth child would be a boy. I asked him how he knew. He said because he was a father he knew. I didn't argue with his prophecies. He knew when the toilets would overflow, or if we would need to stay late to repair a heater or clean after an event. He was a thin man but could carry three times his weight. He had crooked teeth and displayed them freely only in the presence of his children, their teeth girded in metal. He once showed them to me like carefully kept strings of pearls. "Smile," he commanded, and when they didn't, he pulled at the corners of their lips and then grinned himself so I could appreciate the difference. "Order belongs to the wealthy," he said, and we both laughed because that was all we could afford to do.

We became easy friends when he found out I was an islander too but on the other side of the ocean. "I'm Haitian from the Dominican Republic, and my friend here is Tamil from Sri Lanka," he'd say to make sure people knew we didn't fully belong to the countries we came from. His three uncles and aunt had died in the 1937 massacre, and forty-six years later I had lost my home: my wife and two sons. "We are called minorities over there and here," he'd joke.

On a Sunday afternoon, I visited their house with my daughter, Nalini, and the children stood in a line, straight as their teeth, to greet us. They were different sizes but all had Victor's eyes, dark and lean. The oldest was sixteen like Nalini and was the first to welcome us to the house. She brought us soda in tall glasses as her mother sat across from us, her hands pressed lightly against the blue fabric draping her swollen stomach.

The boy was born in February and only a few months later died from a hemorrhage in his brain. I wanted to tell Victor he still had four other beautiful children and that he would manage. But I knew better. And for a few weeks, Victor was quiet, didn't make any more predictions.

On the night of the lunar eclipse, the mother gave birth to another child, and this time blamed the movement of stars and planets when the child was born with miniature arms, tapered like pencils, bitten at the edges. The father laughed and cried while the mother choked on her tongue. In her dreams she stuffed a snakelike creature into a suitcase and sent it floating across the river. The next morning, the child was gone.

I AM DYING. Quietly in bed without much commotion. I don't have much time left, and for that matter time has become quite irrelevant. I find my mind drifting from the past to the present, and sometimes I imagine my wife sitting next to me, scolding me for pissing the bed and drooling into my neck as she wipes the phlegm from my nose. That's mostly untrue because she wouldn't have wanted me to feel shame but rather guilt for leaving her, especially since it's my own doing, my poor habits. The doctors tell me it's because I smoked too much, didn't care for my health. They said I was reckless with my one lung. But really, I'm a coward: I escaped to America as my countrymen wasted away in dug-out trenches, in the open, naked with shrapnel budding from their chests. The war didn't kill me, but the end of the war has. I watch television waiting for news, but my daughter says the civil war ended a year ago and no one is talking about Sri Lanka now. I tell her about the camps in Vavuniya that are still holding Tamil civilians. "Women must change and shower in front of soldiers," I say, and she looks at me. "Nothing has changed," she says, and we are both silent because in a few weeks, months, everything will.

OUTSIDE OUR HOUSE in Wellawatte, Jeganathan was telling me the nature of a spider's life. The art and symmetry of a web. A black spider with gray bands had crawled onto his arm, and he had lowered the arachnid to the ground. "We must respect all living creatures, even the smallest," he said.

This outlook of kindness I had not expected from a young man who had been raised by his grandparents, and who I had once seen trample half-naked under a clothesline, pulling off towels and shirts and turning over pots with the indignation of a tiny conquistador.

"You are young," I told him, and he winced as if I had said something unforgivable. As a doctoral student in the entomology department in Colombo, he must have considered himself wise, knowledgeable in the ways of the world. He never talked of the university protests for the missing students detained without trial under the Prevention of Terrorism Act or the police brutality wielded against the protesters. "Everyone has a grievance," he had told me when I mentioned the young undergraduate in Jaffna who was killed for laughing excessively as a member of parliament passed him in the street.

What I meant to say to him then was that I was nostalgic for the beauty he saw in the world. I could not tell him because he left abruptly in his anger, and Nalini, who watched him keenly all night, followed him to the gate, returned with her face in her hands. From the age of eleven, she had suffered loving him in her adolescent grace.

She was thirty-one when her third child was born. Maybe she had grown tired of her happy vision of a

family or she didn't mind the sight of scaly wings, a cross between an angel and a reptile. They curved from his shoulder blades and instead of trying to rip out his skin, she traced the outlines of his wings, knowing he would not fly away. She was not frightened even when the doctor said they could not remove the wings without disturbing the vertebrae. At home she cut slits into his clothing and sewed cotton slips to cover his wings. This is love, she thought while she washed her son with jasmine-scented soap and watched as he slept on his belly, the wings sailing up and down with his breath.

I FALL ASLEEP while the television is playing, and I wake to soap operas with young people removing their clothes, their naked skin glaring against the screen. I can't find the remote, and I wait for Arjun and Karna to come to my bedside. They arrive separately or if together stand at a distance, these two grandsons of mine. When they were younger, they spoke in the collective. We're hungry. We don't want spinach. We are playing badminton. We are—

DO YOU KNOW the smell of thousands of books burning? The same as a pile of corpses, because fire is the great equalizer. From the second floor of my uncle's home, I thought I heard hundreds of voices screaming from the library, but it was only my own, shredded by the memory of all the childhood visits to Jaffna, where I would sit for hours under the shade of a bookshelf, reading Tamil stories and poems, all turned to ash by the time the soldiers left.

I began to memorize books when I first came to the United States. I picked up a slim volume lying on a table in a coffee shop and read it sixteen times. Even weeks later Kafka's *Meta-*

morphosis left me sobbing in the post office when I recalled the opening paragraph, knowing how much my young friend, the budding entomologist, would have loved to wake up as a giant crustaceous insect with compound vision. And besides, he would have been safer in Sri Lanka if he had grown some antennas and a hard shell. Then he could have sensed danger and wouldn't have looked so dangerous.

Over the years I have trained my mind in the art of word memory. I can read an article twice in the newspaper and remember at least three quarters of it. It's a secret skill, though, and I have never publicly recited anything. My grandsons had simply seen me return home from work and spend the evenings alone with my books, periodicals. They don't know for all these years it was my survival trick, becoming a walking library. But here in bed, my vision is going, only enough to see crude outlines on the television, and then the shapes of past lives.

With my death, will all these books burn too?

As much as I have tried, my grandchildren do not seem interested in safekeeping words. They are forgetful, misplacing the house keys, running after the school bus a minute too late.

"There's only so much we can remember," they tell me. "Sometimes we need to forget something to make room for new memories."

That goes for dying as well.

At the age of three, he showed an affinity with birds. Pigeons would sit on his shoulders, and he wouldn't flinch. He liked to chew on grass, and his mother would find him with green smudged lips, his fingernails coated with mud. His parents named him Santhosham because they thought of their own happiness rather than his. At school, the boy with

wings named happiness smiled too much and was beaten by his classmates, who were bewildered by his perseverance. How can this degenerate keep smiling? Why is happiness so hideous?

WE HAD TWIN boys during the summer solstice, when the daylight lingered. The trees were a golden ash and the dirt streets tinted with copper. As if overnight, Laalini said, everything became brighter because of them. Sooriya, older by a few minutes, and Eashwar, sensitive like a flower. Nalini wanted to hold the two of them as we sat on the verandah, but I was afraid of her carelessness, the way she spilled water when she carried pots inside, unaware of the loss, surprised by her own wet clothes. Laalini sided with Nalini, said the girl was nine years old, almost a young lady. She rested Eashwar on Nalini's lap and then lifted both of them in her arms. Stacked on top of each other, they looked like a Russian doll swaying in the Colombo heat. Before we slept, we bathed the twins. Nalini held a rag to Sooriya's heel and marveled at the brevity of his features. Their mouths open, eager for this world.

IS ANGER LIKE the flesh, does it perish?

A teenage girl with her hair shorn above her ears spoke to me, and I asked her where she lived.

Eelam, she said. The Tamil Nation. The Nation of the Disappeared. The Nation of the Dead.

She closed her eyes, and I recognized her face from a picture I had seen of a young Tiger soldier. She carried a gun and was bald, with an austere beauty.

Next to her face was written the word *Eelam* in bold Tamil letters, as if it were her name. As if she were the homeland for which we were fighting.

Santhosham's wings grew more quickly than they had anticipated. At the age of twelve, they nearly swept the floor. Without feathers, he would not be able to fly. And without flight, they were useless appendages. Still his father was convinced of the aerodynamic potential of his body. "Look, you are like a pterosaur," he said, showing him a book about those ancient dinosaurs, and staring at those colored pages of primordial earth monsters, Santhosham knew that one day he'd go extinct.

NALINI STAYS WITH me in the mornings before she leaves for work. She tells me of the breakfast she cooked and left on my nightstand and her past day in the hospital. I nod my head, avoid speaking, partly because of the pain. As a nurse, she must comfort many patients, but when she speaks, I listen. Because she needs comfort too. She tells me her fears as she straightens the quilt on my bed, trying to bring order to what seems unmanageable. She has had trouble with relationships. Her marriage lasted only five years, and she is afraid to be alone without me. "The problem with a marriage," she says, "is that the love is not unconditional. With a family, it's different."

She has never talked so openly with me, and I wonder what in death frees us to such possibilities.

I move to one side of the bed, and she sits next to me, presses her head against my shoulder. And suddenly again she is no more than a child running to me at night, fearful of the dark walls, her imagination. "Even from soured love," I tell her, "something wonderful can grow."

And I'm glad she has the boys. Let them grow strong with her.

• • •

MY GRANDSONS WARM a sock full of rice in the microwave and keep the soft bundle by my lower back whenever they think I have pain. It is an old tradition, the heat from all those times impressed on that black nylon sock, which itself gives me little relief but sits as a gentle reminder of the hands that brought it. A spoiled sock, full of rice, enough to feed a whole family.

They began to call him the angel of death. First his father went to work, and on returning home, he stepped on a land mine disguised as a frog, which blew off his right leg. Santhosham was only fifteen meters away. Next his mother lost all her teeth one night. The last word she said was her son's name. In school the teacher made him sit in the back of the room after several students complained of inexplicable bloody noses and fevers after bumping into him. Just looking at Santhosham made them feel sick, which had led them to kick him in the gut and punch him between the eyes. Santhosham kept smiling with his bloated, bloody face. He didn't even curse them. No one ever touched the wings except once when a boy took a knife to cut a chunk of flesh but instead only discovered Santhosham's voice, curdling like boiled milk.

I HAVE SAVED old magazines, cassettes I no longer use, any gifts I have received. I kept a pair of blue jeans that were slightly frayed on the bottom for nearly twenty years. When Nalini threw them away, I almost cut all my fingers while chopping onions. "What else do you want to get rid of," I told her, and she just stood there, looking around the house, and I knew she wanted to empty it of everything I loved. *How can you care for these tacky plastic animal figurines from the dollar store?* she'd say.

I mourned those jeans. They were the first pair I bought in the country that fit properly. They had insulated me through the winter when I would find squirrels frozen to death in the schoolyard. The jeans still had value to me, all those shared experiences.

AT THE U.S. embassy in India, a blonde-haired woman stood behind glass and asked me to describe my request for asylum. It was July 1983, and riots had broken out in Colombo.

My uncle from New Jersey was sponsoring my move to the States. As I held Nalini's hand and the small leather pouch with what I had salvaged before the fire, I told the woman we had lost everything. I tugged at Nalini's hand. "My thirteen-year-old daughter is all I have left," I said, and Nalini pulled away, leaving enough space between us for her mother and the twins. We had traveled on a cargo ship first to Jaffna and later paid for a boat to Rameshwaram. I described the crowds, how we stood elbow to elbow with strangers for days. I didn't tell her how I had wanted to throw myself into the ocean, my skin and my eyes still aflame.

"You need to be more specific," the woman said.

I turned away and thought I could not explain, and perhaps I wouldn't have if not for my daughter falling into my arms, her face hidden in my undershirt, which I had worn since the riots, hurrying from my sleep as men entered the house. A yellow curry stain tinted the border of the fabric. How loathsome I must have looked to her in the tidy halls of the embassy in my ruined nightclothes with only one of my children.

"My wife and two sons were killed at my sister-in-law's house in Colombo by a mob."

"Were you there?"

"Yes."

But I wasn't. I was told the story by a neighbor who had witnessed their deaths. He had covered his face and his chest as he approached me, ashamed of the weakness of the human body, the mortality.

The imagination is devious in the way it conjures the truth with unforgiving detail. I saw the red pottu on my wife's forehead like a bull's-eye, and the children whimpering their fears first, unknowingly, dangerously in Tamil, and I tried to hold them in my mind, push away the blur of knives and hands that surrounded them. They might have lived if my wife had not visited her sister. If when I heard rumors of violence, I had kept them close.

I wonder when they left this world if we had sensed their passing, our bodies hidden in the long grass behind the fence as we crawled toward the residence of a young Sinhalese couple that my wife knew very well. We stayed with them for two nights, hidden in their cellar, before heading to the refugee camp. I would later learn the textile mill where I worked as manager was also burned down by a few of the employees. That night, when I turned back, the house was a rope of fire. A man ran out with the television, a dark shadow against the blaze.

The woman wrote a few items on a form. She looked up at me and smiled, out of habit.

Santhosham liked to categorize birds. He could identify twenty-one different species. Sitting outside with his one-legged father and his toothless mother, he would point them out under a cloudless sky. His favorite was the white-headed babbler.

I SAW A man burned alive. They poured gasoline on him and made him lie on the ground, straight as dynamite. "Open your mouth," they said, and he stuck out his tongue like the goddess Kali of Destruction.

DURING THE RIOTS, Jeganathan hid in his boardinghouse. He listened to footsteps and screams that after a few days sounded to him like crickets humming. He drank water from a faucet in the corner of his room twice a day, and let his urine amass and ferment in empty pickle jars. At night cockroaches tiptoed along the walls, and he stayed awake, lying on his back and listening. After a day and a half, the insects looked delectable as raw sweets, and he ate one bug after the other. When a nun found him, he was covered in vomit, disgusted with what he had done—eating those he loved to study. She brought him to the refugee camp at St. Vincent's convent, where we found him.

I told him of what had happened, about the lists of Tamil houses and establishments supplied by the police to mobs. The bodies left beaten on the streets. I did not tell him about Laalini and the twins because I was still hopeful then. Jeganathan seemed unmoved by my words. "What have I done?" he said.

"You will come with us to America."

When we were on the bus headed to the cargo ships, he looked over the damaged city. He was a pensive child and it shames me to think that I never thought of him possessing much strength.

"I will not leave," he said, like there was no choice.

TAMIL STORES IN Nuwara Eliya were burned down. The army supplied the gasoline. The establishment owned by a Sinhalese man married to a Tamil woman was spared. But my parents' shop that had been sold to an elderly Tamil couple was fallen wood and cinder.

Angels don't walk this earth. No one in the history of the village had been born with wings, so

Santhosham was either a messiah or a false prophet. The baker, who was too kind and almost always starving, said of Santhosham: if someone doesn't kill him, the weight of his wings will.

IN 1956 WHEN Sinhala was declared the official language of the country, I decided not to attend university. I had once dreamt of translating Tamil texts into English, and in the end it was language that kept me from that dream. Who would have thought I would be a foreigner in my own homeland? Perhaps I was better off staying on the estate and continuing my father's work at the store, but when my father saw me on my knees sorting through the vegetables, the sight must have disturbed him because soon enough he made arrangements with an old friend in Colombo, and I was named assistant manager of a textile mill. What did I know about garments? I had sewn a button to a sleeve once in desperation.

In America, I worked first behind the register at a Walmart and then as a janitor. At parties with other Tamils from Sri Lanka, I met doctors, lawyers, professors. They would ask me where I was from, and I would say, "Upcountry." With that word, I would see their faces close off, questioning if I were a coolie, a simple laborer from the tea plantation, if I belonged.

MY UNCLE VENKETARAMEN and his wife, Sumathy, told me to remarry and start a new life in America, and I told them that death was the only true rebirth. Sumathy shook her head and said, "There's enough dying happening. You might as well live." She arranged a meeting with a young widow whose husband was shot eighteen times and left by the roadside. She had counted his wounds, she told me. The woman wore jeans and a floral blouse, and drank her tea in tiny sips. She smiled timidly, afraid to claim too much of her own happiness. We chatted through the afternoon. Mostly I rambled into some topic as she listened, responding now and then with nods of her head. Before parting, we stood outside the café. I lit a cigarette and readied myself for the cold. She moved closer to me and plucked the cigarette from between my lips. "You shouldn't be smoking," she said, and the boldness of her movement left me silent, grinning with smoke.

NALINI WANTED TO play the piano, but I chose for her the veena, the instrument of Saraswati. She played roughly, the strings ripping through her skin with each melody, and she showed me her cut hands as though I had inflicted the pain.

"Don't you want to be as lovely as Saraswati?"

"I want to be like Beethoven," she said.

"Why always this Beethoven, Nalini? Do you want to be an ugly old man when you grow up?"

I bought her a keyboard when we found an apartment in Jersey City. It didn't have the right number of keys, but she didn't complain or show much enthusiasm when three months later I returned home with a piano, rolled it four blocks on my own from a yard sale. I think she didn't believe it would work. That it was broken in some way. From that night on, I would wait for the banging of the keys, the uneasy sound of her fingers searching.

Santhosham's mother never told him about the two other boys. They were imaginary sons from another lifetime. Sometimes she saw their shadows dancing along the wall with their hungry bellies while she cooked. "Go away from here," she'd say, and Santhosham would stay up watching the fire burn.

MY NEIGHBOR MR. WU visits me and plays the piano. We never had much need for speaking. He would come by if he needed eggs, and I would cross into his yard and wrestle with his hose. Two old men fumbling into each other's life by accident. He knows I never cared for the piano, but he's stubborn, insistent I hear something beautiful before I pass on, especially since Nalini never plays anymore. Rachmaninoff or Schubert. I don't want to hear any of those dead white men but what choice do I have, bound to a bed, with my mind twirling. But sometimes when I feel kinder about this world, I think death sounds perfectly harmonious, with its unexpected turns, the final crescendo leading to the end, a return.

THE LAST TIME I spoke to Jeganathan was almost six years ago, before he moved to Jaffna with his family. We had lost touch but I followed stories about him online, and I still remember the final article I read of the insect ex-professor. He was unrecognizable to me, and I couldn't stare at his image without thinking of all that I had not witnessed. I showed no one the article, didn't use the Internet for days because some part of me believed Jeganathan had the resilience of a cockroach that could survive anything, a nuclear explosion, the world freezing over, as he hid intact under some rubble. Years later, at the war's end, Nalini asked me who I thought was still alive. We had heard of the perilous journey from the north to safety zones in Mullivaikkal that were no more than a bed of debris and bones, laid out for the purpose of dying.

Nalini has the straight, firm brow of her mother, but nothing in her kept still. I remembered how childhood love never completely dies. I saw Jeganathan standing as a boy with his hands open, two flat palm wings.

Santhosham wanted to move to the city in order to study to become an ornithologist. Out of concern for his safety, his mother and father tied him up

to a chair with rope from the well. He didn't resist and wished them both good night before they slept, kissed each on the cheek. In the morning he was gone; only the rope remained, in three clean pieces on the floor.

"I was always waiting for the third one to leave us too," the mother said and wept.

THERE IS A Sri Lankan restaurant I used to visit close to the school. It is owned by a Sinhalese family. I was a reluctant patron. Whenever I passed the store with the bloody Sri Lankan flag draped across the window, I would spit on the curbside. I don't know if the owners ever saw my face then as I gritted my teeth and fought the urge to piss. One evening Victor and I carried the new heating system into the boiler room and I think that was when the problem with my leg began. I was walking down the street for a gyro when I just collapsed in front of the restaurant. The neon lights of Taste of Sri Lanka blazed above my fallen body, and I just lay there guffawing as the owners, Athula and Chaminda, carried me inside. They rested me on the table and retrieved the cutlery from underneath my sprawled body and I was sure they were going to eat me, but instead they asked me for my name. "I'm Tamil," I said, and they were thrilled when they figured out I was from the island too, which I kept calling Eelam. They sat me down and fed me, and with my mouth full of kottu roti, I might have been crying, everything salty, delicious. I kept eating because I was sure I was having a stroke, delirious and dying, surrounded by two Sinhalese brothers in an empty Sri Lankan restaurant with a Siamese cat watching from the corner of the room. But we never spoke politics so I know I had some of my senses. After that day whenever I passed the restaurant in the evening, the brothers would be waiting at the window precisely for my arrival to drag me inside.

"These Sinhalese men kidnap me and make me eat," I told Nalini over a dinner of spaghetti and canned tomato sauce, which had the distinct taste of metal. With a worm of a noodle hanging from her mouth, she told me to bring her and the kids back food but to feed some to the owners' cat first just in case.

Perhaps I had what they called Stockholm syndrome, and after a while I began to visit the restaurant freely, walking with my own two legs. At the war's end when I rarely left the house, Nalini brought me chili fish curry from the restaurant. She paused before handing over the Styrofoam tray, told me there were banners and balloons all over the place to celebrate the end of the war, the defeat of the Tigers. One of the banners said, "The Terror Is Over."

MY DAUGHTER PRAYS for me when I no longer can, but still the gods cannot leave me and live vividly in my mind. Their lives troubled like ours. Hanuman, the son of Lord Vayu, devours the sun, bright as a mango, and is struck down by Lord Indra, and Lord Vayu of the wind hides and carries away all the air, leaving the world breathless. I focus on that moment: the fallen Monkey God strewn across the ground, the plants and flowers withered, the sky briefly filled with carcasses, the earth browning in the land of the dead.

Santhosham had never traveled far from his village except as a child on those occasional trips to the hospital. He was not anxious climbing onto a bus with strangers jabbing him with looks or later alone in the city when he went to sleep in the park, next to a statue of an English general. He planned to enroll in the university, study birds,

and in the process comprehend his own existence. While he was sleeping he did not know the people in the city despised him. Stories had passed from one clenched mouth to another about a monster, almost human but not enough, feeding on children, defiling virgins. Santhosham woke with his arms and feet tied in bows. He was hauled onto a tree branch, left to hang by his bound wrists. His wings weighed on him like a cloak. They first stripped him to check for any other deformities before deciding how he would disappear from this world. Fire was clean and efficient. They bathed him with gasoline, and because he had kept quiet through everything, they did not anticipate the guttural sound of his voice, a bird cry. As they lit his toes, a curtain of birds descended on the park, only lifting off in the smoke when no men remained.

I SMASHED A liquor bottle in the backyard like a firecracker. The shards sprayed into the night with a sharp glimmer, and I sang out, and Karna clapped his hands beside me.

"Do you want to wake the neighbors?" Nalini said, leaning against the back door.

When she brought us inside, she noticed my pants, the zipper undone, the wetness streaking the edges. Arjun stood behind her, up to her shoulders, his small face mirroring his mother's. She asked me what the children would think from my display.

I looked at them and Karna reached over and held my thumb, and suddenly these grown boys were no older than Eashwar and Sooriya, their fingers grasping for me, spit wet on their lips, telling me to stay.

"Don't shame me," I said, and my voice shook.

• • •

"NALINI, WHAT IS this story supposed to mean?" I asked her once she returned home after a two-day absence and sat at the kitchen table drinking buttermilk, not looking at me of course. "Why do you write these sad, twisted stories about boys with wings and mothers who kill their children?"

She was sixteen, almost old enough to leave me for good, and looking at her, I couldn't understand how time kept going. She didn't want to talk to me but I just sat there, staring at her. She had spent the past nights at Rochelle's apartment above us. Luckily the walls were thin and I could hear the girls laughing, playing music. Those two nights as I waited for her to return home, I went through her room, not out of suspicion but out of desire to find a piece of her that would make me understand. I found some writing titled "A Story of Happiness" in a stack of papers on the desk. I could tell it was a school assignment because the teacher had placed a simple red check mark on the corner of the paper, but as I read the story, I noticed Nalini had spent time on the assignment, probably more time than required. I must have read that story maybe twenty-seven times before she came home. I recited it while I showered, ate breakfast, even began to murmur lines before I fell asleep. I don't know why I was so determined to keep those words. Maybe I thought something in that story could save us both.

"Who is Santhosham supposed to be?"

Nalini shrugged and rubbed a white spot on the table.

"And why all these birds?"

"Maybe he's your childhood friend," she said.

"My friend."

"Maybe it's me."

"The two dead boys in the beginning."

She shook her head and leaned forward. "Maybe he's just all of us."

"But why name this 'A Story of Happiness' when there's nothing happy about it?"

Her lower lip shivered and she bit into it to kill the feeling. "Why do a few sad events have to make a whole life unhappy?"

She looked at me, and I turned away.

"AMMAPPA," ARJUN SAYS, "are you sleeping?" I stir slowly, reach into my body with reluctance. Sitting on a chair, he is bent forward, his hand near my mouth, and when I open my eyes fully, he leans back quickly and talks of the weather as he stares at the rice sock squirming on his lap.

"Do I look dead to you?" I say.

He doesn't answer, and I wonder how easy it is for him to imagine a world without me.

Stories return to the village of a winged man who flew off with the birds. But what astonished the town was a single detail before the flight. For all those who thought Santhosham was a eunuch, they struggled to believe angels could have penises.

MY DAUGHTER MARRIED an Indian man, a Punjabi. He was born and raised in New Jersey, so I suppose that makes him an American man. He would go by Mo, but I only knew him as Mohinder. He attended high school and then college with Nalini, and in that time, he proved to be average not only in his studies but in his growth, surpassing Nalini's height only in his senior year. He came consistently to our apartment, and he looked harmless with his spectacles and his starched white shirts. At dinner, he once sat and told me all about the business of mortgages and problems of high interest rates, perhaps to impress me. Nalini called him a bore, and as I listened to him,

I could see how those words affected his manner, tightened his lips. His vulnerability did not necessarily make me fond of him but it made me mind him less. On the one occasion I discussed Sri Lankan politics with him, I said in half seriousness, "The only thing the Sri Lankan government and the Tamil Tigers could agree on was that Indian peacekeeping troops needed to leave," and I pointed at him, maybe because I knew he would not leave, that he would marry my daughter. Only years later would those words return to me as I stood on the porch and watched my daughter admire the newly planted lilies with Arjun beside her. Turning to me, she smiled, too expectant with her second child to show sorrow.

I TELL MY grandsons that I'm lucky to die this way. "Not everyone has the privilege to die in the comfort of a bed, in old age," I say, but they're not listening, and I want to keep on speaking to them. "I'm lucky," I repeat, and Karna looks worried, holding my hand. Arjun searches the medical box as he curses at the phone.

The birds sang and sang, and he—

THE OFFICE OF MISSING PERSONS

ON THE NIGHT HIS ELDER SON went missing, V. S. Jeganathan dissected a monarch butterfly. He measured the span of the wings three times before his younger son and wife returned to his study with the same worried expressions. Outside the clothes on the laundry line inflated and danced in the breeze. "I'll leave for the capital tonight," he said, reaching for his blazer, the fabric squeezed between a fortress of boxes, still unpacked after all these years.

"Don't you disappear too," his wife said.

Near midnight he climbed onto the bus in Thirunelveli and as he held out his fare, he became aware of the weight of his hand, the conductor's hesitation before accepting his payment. The man's face folded in disgust. Only then did Jeganathan notice the crushed fragments of wings, insect legs sticking to his fingertips.

The main room of the police station was painted a sunny yellow. A bronze statue of the Buddha greeted him when he entered and partially hid the crack that ran down the center of the front wall, where a policeman sat at his desk hunched over an open magazine. The man was exceptionally thin except for his belly, which hung like a rice sack so even the crook of his neck seemed to bow. He was too busy grazing his fingers against an advertisement of a woman sniffing perfume to see him, and when Jeganathan first spoke, the officer looked up perturbed, his open hand lightly smacking the printed lady.

Holding out a school photograph, Jeganathan began to speak Sinhala in a slow, precise manner as if he were walking on a tightrope, his son's life caught in the balance of enunciating a language he had not needed to speak for the past three years living up in the north. As he described Jeevan's disappearance, the officer tapped his fingers together and stared at framed portraits of President Mahinda Rajapaksa and the ex-president Chandrika Kumaratunga hanging from the wall.

The officer asked for Jeganathan's son's name and he knew it was a trick. He needed his name to find him and then have reason not to find him.

The officer placed his gold wire-rimmed glasses on his face. He opened a black binder, wet his thumb on the inside of his lip, and glanced over the papers. He filled in Jeevan's information on a sheet alongside other names. "Where was he headed?" he asked.

Jeganathan paused. "He did not return home after his studies."

"These young Tamil boys always getting into trouble. They don't know how to be proper citizens," the officer said and scratched something on the paper in blue ink. Jeganathan remembered his younger boy, Prem, shaking on the floor as they questioned him, his eyes flushed with tears as he cut through the bond of the womb and revealed the trip Jeevan had planned that night with Amutha to the local Shiva shrine, and before then all their meetings under the neem trees by the abandoned pharmacy, the way his brother unraveled her braid, tied her hair around his hand like a bandage.

The officer asked for a description of the missing boy beyond the photograph. Jeganathan lifted his hands and attempted to re-create Jeevan for the officer, but under the dim fluorescent light, any conjuring was hopeless. In the end, the officer wrote: *17 years old, 181 centimeters, 76 kilograms, birthmark on right arm.*

"When will the search begin?"

"It has already begun," the officer said.

"How can that be? I just got here."

The officer waved off the question and proceeded to speak, pointing a finger at Jeganathan's head like a pistol. "We will tell you if we find him."

Outside the police station was a truck filled with goats. They cried out to him, and Jeganathan, with the collar of his shirt twisted and his hair uncombed, stood next to the vehicle as the creatures nibbled on the pasture of his head.

JEGANATHAN WORKED AS an entomologist. He was not prone to chatting except in the lecture halls in front of his students, talking of what he loved best. He was fastidious with what he could control, his ironed suits and finely trimmed mustache, the way he recorded his work in his notebook, the column for wingspan blank until he measured the specimen three times.

He had never been militant. He joked about dueling other entomologists like William de Alwis, the Sri Lankan butterfly man, because they seemed harmless. In keeping company with insects, he had avoided addressing the war altogether, though his wife disagreed on that matter. In her eyes, he was a man so dedicated to his work that he was willing to get both his legs blown off for some dung-eating insects.

"Weren't you almost killed by a mob in Colombo? And look, we're still here in this country," his wife said after hearing of his job transfer from the capital to up north. "I thought by marrying a professor we'd end up in Toronto, Sydney, London, anywhere better, and now you want to take me to Jaffna. Do you want to get us deeper into this war?"

Jeganathan had decided to transfer to Jaffna not because of politics but because of a discovery. While praying in the Murugan temple in Nallur, he saw a blue beetle skitter across the floor. The strange wings and streaks along its abdomen forced him to his knees, and he crawled after the specimen. He carried the beetle in a jar all the way back to his office in the capital. After his examinations, he suspected he had discovered a new species. He named the insect—*Nicrophorus m. kumaratunga*—after the president at the time, and when questioned by officials what the *m* stood for, he said, Madame, not the Hindu deity Lord Muruga. While officials hassled other Tamil intellectuals at the university, they did not bother with him, the professor whose blue-winged insect talisman granted him a level of immunity.

Jeganathan believed there were more new species in Jaffna. His blue-winged beetle was only the beginning. But he had no way to prove his claims. All his possible theories had holes or perhaps bullet wounds. He could not understand anything, day or night, without positioning himself in relation to the movement of the war. Over the years, he had chronicled every massacre, every fight as potential sights of discovery. He carried with him maps of Jaffna and the northeast with silver pins pricked into specific latitudinal and longitudinal coordinates. He had been widely regarded as the president's Insect Man because his findings had brought the country modest international recognition. The government, eager for him to further his research, allowed him access to sites with ecological disturbances. Walking through a village after a fresh killing, Jeganathan couldn't help but feel nervous as the army waited for him to finish his bug investigation before eradicating the site. He'd keep his eyes low to the ground, trying to overlook humanlike material, a necklace, a charred shoe, a three-fingered hand pointing in the direction of the sky. He had trained his eyes to look so closely for the minuscule he could obscure his vision.

Of his undisclosed theories, he kept returning to two of them, both unlikely. One dealt more with evolution, the war cutting through the landscape, creating barriers between existing species and forcing a divergence; still, a few decades was hardly enough time for such a dramatic transformation. Maybe war altered the nature of time: minutes could become years.

The second theory was more provocative, belonging to the realm of science fiction, but still possible. The beetles might have been genetically engineered and strategically dropped around Jaffna by the military. Though not known to be aggressive to humans, some beetles, like the bombardier beetle, unleashed a gaseous cocktail that burned and blistered the skin. Jeganathan wondered if his blue-winged beetles possessed a more secretive way to release toxins, if the military had developed a slow, gradual way to kill without raising alarm. This line of thinking left him paranoid. Because if he was the president's Insect Man, then he was being used as the smiling puppet of the project, bringing prestige to the machinery killing his own people.

When he had searched through the village of Mirusuvil soon after the massacre, he found an old man shivering in a chicken coop. "They took all my chickens, three hundred," he said. "The soldiers." He had lost his entire extended family, and lying in chicken shit, he held on to a handful of dirty feathers. The light from the roof flickered across the absence.

AFTER JEGANATHAN'S SON went missing, he would keep long hours in his study. He spoke to no one. Insects floating in glass jars stared at him from the shelves. Only his younger son visited him in the evenings with a cup of tea, which his wife sent, brimming with her bitterness. Two teaspoons of salt instead of sugar mixed in. He drank the potion, wanting this waiting to end and fearing the end. He had already visited Amutha's house. The girl was distraught, her mother told him, vomiting everywhere. When Jeganathan saw her, she was crumpled on a cot. "I don't think I will recover," she said. The last time she had seen Jeevan was outside her home; he had tossed a rock into a gutted car and cracked the window.

When Jeganathan's wife asked about Amutha, he could hear the beginnings of concern plummet into anger for this girl who seduced her son and led him out late at night where he shouldn't have been in the first place.

Already neighbors kept their distance. They never liked the family from the capital but now their displeasure had proper reason. Misfortune spread and they needed to protect themselves. Not even beggars stopped by the house. As if surrendering to the neighbors' vision of decay, his wife did not clean, kept everything as it was the day of their son's absence. An empty tumbler on Jeevan's nightstand remained though flies clung to the metal rim, still sticky with lime juice.

In the lecture hall, Jeganathan saw his son everywhere. He was falling asleep in the middle of a lesson. He was nervously flirting with a girl outside the canteen. He was reading a book under the giant neem tree in the courtyard. His students with their round, inquisitive faces looked up at him, filled with urgency to know just like his own son, reading Khalil Gibran late at night with the lantern, underlining sentences. *How noble is the sad heart who would sing a joyous song with joyous hearts.*

Jeevan was a popular student, friends with both boys and girls. His teachers called him a natural leader, talkative and compassionate. It thrilled Jeganathan to hear those words about his son and watch the confident way he moved through the world. Unlike his son, Jeganathan was timid, never raised his hand as a student, and preferred conversing with his insects rather than his colleagues. But he loved talking about his son, standing next to Jeevan and telling people he was *his* father. Though Jeevan looked more like his mother, Jeganathan's sperm was half the beginning, and the fact excited him because somewhere deep within himself he too carried hidden talents, possibilities. And the fact also made him anxious because if he was prudent, his son was reckless, if he was soft-spoken, his son was outspoken. Jeganathan had advised his sons to stay inconspicuous as insects. Shouldn't he have known Jeevan would be in danger?

Jeganathan had contacted the local police, lodged cases in the capital, but had heard nothing. Over the phone, one official asked him if he was sure his son existed, that maybe he just had one son. And for a brief stretch of a sound wave, he wanted to believe it—he had only one son in his happy family with his happy insects—and then he screamed at the man, calling him a donkey-fucking, ten-handed pervert.

On the fifth day of his son's absence, Jeganathan did not return to the university. He sat in his undershirt at the table in the kitchen while his wife shredded carrots.

"We shouldn't have come here," she said.

Jeganathan's hair was uncombed, his legs knotted under him. "This could have happened even in Colombo." He covered his eyes. "We should have left long ago."

JEGANATHAN'S FRIEND NADARAJAH was a journalist who worked for a small newspaper, *Red Earth*, in Valvettithurai. He would inform Jeganathan about any recent massacres in the area. Claymore attacks by the Deep Penetration Unit often left the earth ripped open. *Maybe there are metallic insects under the surface with shrapnel exoskeletons*, he wrote to Jeganathan on the day a school bus hit one of the mines. Nadarajah had wanted to become a physicist and study the laws of nature. He remembered the formula for the force of gravity when he saw a man's head chopped and thrown into the sky like a football, and later he wrote about the incident for the local paper, knowing then there was no formula for the trajectory of his future. After Nadarajah reported on a nineteen-year-old Tamil girl who was raped by six soldiers and thrown into a well, he went missing the next afternoon. His body was found outside the police station, his skull crushed.

Nadarajah also had a daughter named Amutha.

She was two years younger than Jeevan and bold like her father in her own quiet way. Jeganathan had once seen her standing at the bus stop with a needle and thread in hand, offering to sew a boy's torn shirt in full public display. She had returned from a wedding, and the jasmines in her hair clung to the gate behind her as if the flowers had grown from the metal, contained hints of rust. Perhaps that was what his son saw in her, after all those visits to the house, the daughter of his father's dead friend. They'd sit side by side, and Jeevan would press his hand over hers in a small gesture of comfort. On more than one occasion Jeganathan had heard Amutha call Jeevan brother.

Jeganathan visited her in the evenings with Prem. "She is still ill," her mother would say, serving them a tray of sweets. "She can't keep food down."

Prem would eat what Amutha couldn't, as if he were helping her with this simple act. With Jeevan's absence, Jeganathan began to see his younger son with a new alertness. He noticed the way he leaned his weight to his right side, a habit he must have picked up from his brother, just like his watchfulness for Amutha. When she touched her throat, Prem knew to bring her a tumbler of water. Seven years younger, he moved with the bearing of another life.

Before saying farewell, Jeganathan bought perfume Amutha's mother made in the kitchen. It was more of an herbal broth, an antidote to the cruelties of life.

"Keep the rest," Jeganathan said and handed her enough money to buy seven bottles but only took one. She shook her head, feigned reluctance like she always did, before pocketing it. Jeganathan's wife had a drawer full of these perfume bottles of sage and neem leaves. His wife greeted these gifts with dark laughter. *At least this scent will protect me from the soldiers.*

On the eighth day of his son's disappearance, Jeganathan returned to the university, and during the lecture he abruptly went silent. He was speaking on pheromones when his voice vanished. His mouth snapping open like a fish unsure how to breathe.

"Professor," a student called out, and Jeganathan ran for the toilet, poured water on his head, gasping.

The next afternoon he marched around town, calling out his son's name and the date of his disappearance. Outside the university, he sat on the grass underneath the neem tree and called for justice. Neighbors pitied him but privately called him selfish. "How about my nephew?" an old woman with two silver-colored teeth asked. Others cried: *How about my son? How about my daughter? How about my sister? How about my brother-in-law?* They all loved people who were born to disappear.

AFTER TWO WEEKS of Jeganathan's protesting, the university board members dismissed him from his post. Only temporarily, they assured him. They were on his side. Jeganathan did not seem alarmed by the news as he sat by Prem's bedside recalling the incident. He asked Prem to help him carry his belongings from his office at the university.

"We will not tell Amma too soon," he said. He pushed his head closer to the window to admire the garden. "The cicadas are especially noisy tonight. No one likes that."

At the university Prem carried a box of books and Jeganathan held a tank with his prized insects. They paused at the neem tree and Jeganathan checked his watch. He cleared his throat and pulled out a paper from his pocket. With a mechanical precision, he folded his legs, angled his head, and recited Jeevan's name along with others: a collection of strangers.

By late afternoon three police officers approached them.

"Don't you be doing this anymore," one of the officers said. "It's our job to find your son."

The uniforms hung loosely on them like extra skin. They were young and eager, the same age as Jeganathan's students. An officer bent to his knees and touched the glass tank with a black rod and turned his eyes to Jeganathan. He rolled the rod in his hand as he examined Jeganathan's long, lean face. A dog barked and the officer turned away and then stared at the other two men, who wore their rifles slung to their sides like school bags. The two officers stepped a few meters back, jumped over a strip of weeds. When a group of girls passed, the officer thrust his hand back and shattered the tank. The girls pushed closer to one another and yelled. Scorpions and horned centipedes raced across the grass.

Jeganathan watched his beloved creatures and then looked at the officers. "Poisonous," he said, and for a moment the officers looked concerned. But their faces settled, and one mouth opened for the three and said, "So be it."

MONARCH BUTTERFLIES USED the sun to navigate their journey, but on cloudy days, they became tiny compasses and could follow the earth's magnetic field. Jeganathan thought of the butterflies when he imagined his son blindfolded and handcuffed in a dark room, sensing home in a pitch beyond human frequency.

Amutha began to visit the house in the evenings after her mother napped. She said she came to inquire about Jeevan, but there was never news. She simply drank tea and played card games with Prem. Jeganathan's wife did not speak with her but watched her from a distance. Each time Amutha stayed a little longer, offering to help chop vegetables or hang the laundry or chase off mosquitoes, and by then Jeganathan's wife could not resist the little solace of female company. After a meal, Amutha ate slivers of butter and spoons of sugar. When Jeganathan saw her licking her fingers alone in the kitchen, he asked her if she was still hungry.

"I'm pregnant," she said and wiped her hands against her belly.

"How long?"

"Maybe over a month." She paused and looked out the window. "Are you not angry?"

Jeganathan didn't say anything, but his mouth was open. He knew he was crying because he could taste the unending sea. *His sperm, his sperm,* he sobbed while Amutha kept apologizing, *I'm sorry, I'm sorry.* Everything that mattered and did not matter about his son resided in the knowledge dug deep within an invisible bean sprout created in the act of love. Unbelievable was the human body, with all its orifices and extensions. Right then he wished he could talk to his boy, tell him he was twenty-eight, practically a decade older, when he first touched a woman. Oh god, they were so remarkably different, weren't they?

Amutha showed him a baby shirt she had sewn two years ago, as if she had always known she'd become a mother before becoming a wife.

"You are too young," Jeganathan said.

"But we age like dogs here. I'm actually over a hundred years old."

Jeganathan did not tell his wife about the baby. She was already too absorbed in the loss of her baby, her seventeen-year-old baby, and waking in the middle of the night, she chose to disregard time, indifferent to the numbers on a calendar or the portions of a day. Instead she chose to sit, rest, drown in a timeless moment. What would nine months mean to her? Waiting for a baby that was Jeevan's but not Jeevan.

Over the weeks Jeganathan had become a bit of an eccentric celebrity to the Tamil community abroad. An acquaintance had written about him online on his semipopular blog, *Thiru-4Life.* But it was the photograph of Jeganathan with his eyes bulging from his sockets, his beard peppered with food remains as fruit flies circled near him, and then the caption, "Daily Protests of the Insect Professor," that must have captured the moral disgust of a global audience. Disbelief that a professor who studied insects could transform into an insect or a vagabond.

Jeganathan no longer had his university job, and his wife claimed he had turned their family into first-class beggars. "We get our charity in the mail," she said as she ripped open internationally stamped envelopes from sympathetic members of the Tamil Diaspora. "I bought this fish because of a Mr. Soundarajan from Brooklyn."

His students remained loyal to their old professor. Though they had slept through most of his lectures, they chanted by him, followed his breathing like he was a guru. They had written the names of the missing on their bodies, and before chanting, Jeganathan would listen to the clamor of their voices:

"Do you remember when Ravichandran was jacking himself off while shelling was falling from the sky?"

"Because he wanted his end to be orgasmic."

"But no one can maintain an erection when they think they are about to die."

"You don't understand, he was beyond fear. It was divine."

"The two separate incidents are meaningless unless they overlap."

"Like a collage of images."

"Isn't that a metaphor?"

War had seeped into the meaning of everything. Forty-seven students and one insect ex-professor sitting cross-legged and calling for the return of the disappeared were terrorists in training according to the reports from the central government. That week the United Nations Working Group on Enforced or Involuntary Disappearances also released a report ranking Sri Lanka as the country with the second-highest number of disappearances. In response, the press secretary, a petite man with white hair spraying out of his ears, raised his hands and spoke with the euphoria and confusion of a drunkard in a bar fight.

"When was the last time we were number two in the whole world," he said. "Imagine that we beat countries like Iran and Sudan. Sooner or later, we'll take down the number one champ. Iraq, we're coming for you!"

Before the press secretary's display, public outrage in the

capital over the report was minimal or nonexistent, but after such a blabbering mess, even officials called for a response, and the Office of Missing Persons was created. The sole purpose of the office was to track down the disappeared. Leaflets were dropped in Jaffna and the northeast of the country describing the role of the office, the various branches located in different towns. The cardamom-colored papers floated down and drifted past unsuspecting faces. A man riding his bicycle felt the paper cut the back of his ear and he shrieked, thinking he had been shot.

At the office, people demanded clarification. The one, nameless clerk struggled to follow their Tamil. He was only an assistant to the officials overseeing the disappearances. He just recorded information, he insisted.

"Mr. Missing Assistant, what is the difference between the police station and this office?"

"The police are going after present crimes."

"Mr. Missing Assistant, are these disappearances past crimes?"

"We have no evidence at the moment to call them crimes. After proper investigation, we can evaluate these claims more fully."

"Mr. Missing Assistant, doesn't every crime become part of the past once it is committed?"

"We will review these alleged crimes, but remember fault has not been allocated. If someone falls into a hole and disappears, whose fault is that? If two hundred or three thousand people fall into the same hole, maybe it's their own fault. They should have been more careful."

Though mistrustful of any new or old form of bureaucracy, Jeganathan reported his son's disappearance to the Office of Missing Persons and watched as the information was lost in dark stacks cowering in the corner of the room. He left feeling as if his son had further disappeared.

At night his wife held him for the first time in years. She tried to cradle him like an infant. "There, there, my treasure," she cooed at him as he cried.

He didn't tell her about the latest death threat he received. A note perfumed with urine and a few words about his testicles being chopped off. He noticed the differences in the handwritings in the notes he had received over the weeks, and at night he wondered if he would rather be executed by someone with impeccable penmanship or someone who was so sloppy that they even misspelled his name. Which death would be less painful?

Most often he did not think of his own passing because he had already accepted the fact that he would die unexpectedly without much say in the matter. He lived for that singular moment of the day, during protests with the students, when the sun struck their backsides and their shadows formed one great ink-stained creature on the lawn. Mesmerized by this circumstantial discovery, Jeganathan would wonder if all his time crawling on the earth, being bitten and stung, he had been searching for this mythic arthropod. Countless limbs and perturbing chatter. The unceasing absence of silence.

While the Office of Missing Persons stayed unabashedly quiet, people grew louder, banging on the door, throwing their voices like rocks. An artist whose father and four siblings had disappeared believed the structure functioned as a burial chamber, a place to inter memories and forget. Since the artist drank most days, lived unemployed for years with his art of molded cow dung and lilies, acting as the only corporeal onus for his single mother, who already had to lug the missing with her, people didn't pay him much mind. But a few weeks later, as the missing accumulated, people suddenly began to forget details of their loved ones. Did he have an overbite or an underbite? Would he drool when he kissed me? Where did he have that ugly birthmark shaped like an island?

One evening right after sunset, a group trying to unforget burned down the Office of Missing Persons. Ash thickened the air and in a matter of a few hours, their memories felt safe, contained within them. Overnight officials at the capital learned that the Office of Missing Persons had disappeared or, more aptly, was cremated. In secret government cables, it was recorded that the deputy of defense, known for his religious devotion—offering alms and praise to every monk he passed—said: *Look at what these fuckers do with our kindness. We'll show them how to really disappear.*

Jeganathan was unaware of the events surrounding the night. He was home in his study, not working but reviewing the inventory of his life. Dead insects, some textbooks from university, a single family photo from a trip to a tea estate in Nuwara Eliya. From the beginning, he had never settled in; most of his boxes remained packed, as if he had always anticipated his future departure.

He could hear his wife and son talking in the kitchen, their voices blending into one as an MGR song fried on someone's radio. He walked from room to room without any intention of staying but found himself seated at Jeevan's desk, his hands turning the pages of his sky blue notebook. Some pages had math equations, paragraphs on biology, doodles of eyes and upside-down pyramids. Hidden in the right-hand corner of the second-to-last page he found a poem:

plant a shard of shrapnel and it will
grow into our lives. a limbless boy
learned to dance by crawling.
but you cut a jackfruit not knowing

what was inside,
your father's head, an army of ants,

fearless,
you call my name
and do not tremble
like i do in wonder how
my hands do not explode when
i hold you—that life could be so sweet.

My son.

AN OLD MAN filed a case at the Office of Missing Persons that his village had disappeared. He had returned from a trip to the south and nothing remained except a big hole in the earth. This was the nearest Office of Missing Persons he could find.

"Perhaps your village has been relocated?" a clerk said.

"To where?"

"You must wait and see."

The old man sat outside under the noon sun. He had nowhere to go, nothing to do but to wait. When the clerk left in the evening, he locked up the office and found the old man dead, his shirt wrapped around his head, and a dog licking at his toes.

WHEN WE WERE CHILDREN

THREE WEEKS BEFORE DILRAJ ARRIVED, Nalini began receiving postcards from Rochelle from places around the world. London, Milan, Berlin. She was traveling for six months with a Norwegian businessman named Adrian whom she met at a bar in Atlantic City. "It's almost like taking maternity leave," she had told Nalini, though the school district probably wouldn't pay her. Nalini had warned her against trusting a stranger, especially one willing to spend so much money on her, but Rochelle had laughed over the phone, her voice already intoxicated. "At least our mixed Norwegian children will be rich."

In the afternoon a postcard arrived from Amsterdam with a picture of Vincent van Gogh's sunflowers. It was famous, of course, but Nalini felt excited imagining Rochelle in the museum standing in front of the real painting, a work of art that Dilraj might have called overrated. Rochelle had only jotted a few lines, mentioned the cobblestone roads and the surplus of bicycles. Since it was nearing the holidays, the end of October, she couldn't help but notice these ugly, colonial images of Saint Nicholas's helper, Zwarte Piet. Rochelle was glad Adrian was not Dutch because when they had children, he might call them something awful, which she couldn't forgive.

Nalini's address was written in neat block letters: 126 North Lane, Louisville, Kentucky. It looked unrecognizable to her, that address, even after five years. She wondered if Rochelle felt that too, writing it on the postcard, to a place she had never planned to visit.

Dilraj was still asleep on the sofa bed, his right leg dangling over the edge. Only after twelve hours of sleep, half the day tucked under him, would he wake restless, finding ways to pester her about finishing college or instructing her to play the piano. She knew grief made you act out in strange ways so she complied. She pulled out anatomy and biochemistry textbooks packed away under her bed and pretended to study. Or, sitting at the piano, she played a simple melody. Last week he baked a spinach pie and she could still taste the bland crunch of eggshells and no salt.

Unlike her brother-in-law, her husband had been quieter in his mourning. After they had thrown his mother's ashes into the Atlantic Ocean, he had cursed and mumbled to himself, "I'm an orphan." She wanted to console him, tell him she understood what it was like to lose a mother, but instead she had said, "Twenty-six is too old to be an orphan," as she watched the waves bounce along.

Mohinder returned to his work as an accountant across the Ohio River and because of his brother's persistence, Dilraj closed up the store in Jersey City and stayed with them. "Just don't like the idea of you living there alone," her husband had told Dilraj, holding his younger brother's hand.

They didn't look much alike, except for the slender shape of their noses and the protrusion of their cheeks. Mohinder was now slightly taller than Dilraj, though as children Dilraj towered over him. They both had the same close-lipped smile.

While Dilraj slept, she noticed changes in him, how his body had whittled down to bones. Under his eyes were dark cups and he wiped away any wetness that collected when he woke. He sounded cheerful, but she could sense his anxiousness in the way his clothes hung on him, only natural, she supposed, after his mother's sudden passing.

She cared for him the best she could, made sure he ate, watched him until his plate was clean. He ate slowly but with a hunger that she imagined was fed by the months of surviving off snacks from the convenience store while he worked.

After he woke, she showed him the postcard from Rochelle, and he weighed the paper in his hand before flipping it over.

"Rochelle is seeing the world like she said she would," Dilraj said, flattening the card with his palm.

"I think she's a fool to go chasing a man around."

"From what I hear, it sounds like they are traveling together."

Nalini cleared the table and ran the faucet. She could feel his eyes on her, and she wanted to turn and throw a dish at him. How long did she have to accommodate his grief? But when she thought of him alone in his parents' apartment, working at his family's convenience store, she felt ashamed. He had stayed in Jersey while they left. They had abandoned him along with her father.

She soaked her fingers in the soapy water and let them turn old. Dilraj had opened the patio door and was sitting in the backyard. Through the oval window above the sink, she could see him seated with his arms crossed behind his head in a landscape painting, the evergreen and maple trees framing the image. Sudden strokes of birds on slender branches cut the sky into polygons. For a moment, staring at this piece of her life, she felt an overwhelming peacefulness and knew she was where she was meant to be. She wished she could carry this feeling like a candle from the kitchen to the bedroom, and at night when she woke fearful and uncertain, she would see the light and know she was home.

When they first moved to the outskirts of Louisville five years ago, Mohinder spent most of his time outdoors, admiring the French windows, the burgundy brick veneer, as if astonished by their modest fortune of owning a house. She tried working her way through it, mopping and dusting, in hopes she would come to form an attachment to the place. During the second week, when she first moved the stove, she discovered shriveled lemons. They were hidden everywhere, in the corners of closets and on top of light fixtures. Dried halves, the color of jaundice, stared at her with the grim promise of empty eye sockets. "The house was cheap because it's cursed," she had told Mohinder, who tried to reassure her, pressing his hand against her belly to calm the baby.

She wondered if the Mexican grandmother who had lived in the house had been warding off some evil eye, and she began performing her own rituals. She circled herself with a handful of salt in the mornings and chopped up fruits like oranges, apples, and lemons and left them deep in the backyard, where Mohinder could not see. She once told him about the dead raccoon she found in the trash, and he seemed unbothered until she told him how she had buried the creature in the front yard by the ferns and the petunias. He thought the act strange, primordial for their suburban neighborhood. "We're not the Iqbals," he said, mentioning the Pakistani couple ten miles away who were found guilty of torturing their maid.

Mohinder had been serious even as a child, striving for respectability; his father's early death forced him to grow up early, and at thirteen, he wrote his mother's checks and helped her with taxes. Still he surprised Nalini by buying her impractical gifts like large magnetic spoons and a clock that frequently paused to show the wrong time. She played along as he woke an hour earlier each day until all they could see was darkness and he spent the time awake with her, missing a whole day of work. His sudden flashes of silliness amused her, and she thought swayed her into marriage, even if it was only the matter of the baby.

When it was almost three o'clock, she wiped her wet hands against her shirt and grabbed her purse. Locking the front door, she could hear Dilraj singing from the backyard as she left to pick up Arjun from school.

THEY ALL HAD lived in the same apartment complex in Jersey City. Manchester Flats. It was a square beige building, stained with watermarks, formerly a home for senior citizens sane enough to live by themselves. Nalini knew the place was inexpensive because anything named after foreign European cities meant there were probably rodents hiding in the walls and mildew in the shower. "Refugees can't be picky, and at least we're making our way up," her father had said as they moved everything they had while living in Uncle Venketaramen's basement to a first-floor apartment that faced two warehouses and a drugstore.

Rochelle lived in the apartment above and in the evenings Nalini listened to the family sit down for dinner, their voices full of chatter, while below she ate fried eggs and rice, her father asleep on the couch next to the television. She didn't think Rochelle noticed her subterranean existence until one day returning from school Rochelle called out her name as they crossed the pavement to the apartment complex. "You from Sri Lanka," she said and continued to tell Nalini how she herself might be from Nigeria. Over the months, while Nalini distanced herself from her countrymen, Rochelle tried to reclaim hers, ancestors who were kidnapped and shackled across the ocean. "I'm from nowhere but here," she said, and Nalini jumbled her words. "I'm here but from nowhere."

They were both thirteen but Rochelle was older by seven months, so naturally Rochelle played the teacher and Nalini the diligent student, her hair braided to the center of her spine, her floral frocks mushrooming around her whenever she sat. In the kitchen Rochelle cut off Nalini's braids using her mother's meat knife and cutting board, leaving her hair serrated to her shoulders. Digging through her clothes, Rochelle found old pairs of jeans, faded but still wearable. Before long, Nalini practiced playing air guitar with her teeth like Jimi Hendrix and no one called her Pococuntis.

Mohinder and Dilraj lived down the hall from Rochelle. Mohinder was fourteen and Dilraj was twelve. Their family's convenience store was five blocks away, near the train tracks that carried uninteresting objects like metal beams and canisters of oil but never people. Because they had nowhere else to go, Rochelle and Nalini hung around the store with the boys, checking if anyone stole and nibbling on bags of Fritos as their mother endured behind the register. "My back aches and I'm short of breath," she'd tell the girls and, unable to resist sharing, she'd even show them where she had fractured her foot years ago when her husband was still alive.

A POSTCARD ARRIVED from Greece, slightly damp, as if it had washed up from the image of the coastline. The temperature had dropped close to freezing in Louisville and Nalini kept looking at the photograph to warm herself. As girls, they would sunbathe on a rectangular block of grass outside the apartment complex and Rochelle's mother would come to the balcony every ten minutes, telling them they were both already dark, couldn't get any darker than radioactive.

By the time Mohinder returned from work, Nalini had finished with dinner while Arjun and Dilraj huddled inside a fort of sofa cushions, whispering like the last two living humans in the world. They had shortened their names to the last syllables, Jun and Raj, calling out to each other in a sound to know what they shared, deep as blood.

When they all sat at the table, Nalini showed everyone the postcard.

"From certain angles, it almost looks like the Jersey Shore," Dilraj said, holding the card an arm's length away.

Mohinder rolled up his sleeves. "Makes sense because you're almost blind."

"Which must heighten my other senses." He licked the sauce from the corner of his lips.

Mohinder loosened his tie and apologized to Nalini for having to deal with his senseless, skeletal brother all day. She wanted to reach over and wipe the dried crust near his nose but she remembered the night before lying underneath him, her body losing mass. He was worried about his brother, believed he was wasting his chemistry degree in a convenience store. "We were robbed so many times and my parents still never sold it," he had said as she felt the sweat sliding between them. "I'm sorry," she said and thought how she had no degree at all, her pregnancy put an end to that, along with this house they had purchased, far from the community college she had planned to attend.

She could tell Mohinder wanted to speak to Dilraj on these matters over dinner, and his brother must have sensed this too because he took Nalini's hand and said they had been practicing for over a week. In the living room Nalini sat by the piano with Dilraj next to her on the bench. She didn't want to play, and felt suddenly shy at the idea of having Mohinder listen. She no longer possessed the musical talent of her adolescence, which never really amounted to much. First prodding the keyboard her father had purchased and then the out-of-tune piano he bought off some street corner for twenty-five dollars and a carton of cigarettes. Everything in her life—down to the men's navy jacket she wore from the Salvation Army for a whole winter in high school—felt like a compromise. When Mohinder had insisted she bring the piano with her from New Jersey for memory's sake, Nalini paused and tried to recall the last time he spoke with such sentimentality; in retaliation, she mentioned efficiency, complained about the size, the unfeasibility of wheeling that musical monstrosity. "It'll be good for the baby to hear his mother," he said. Now she remembered how she sounded when she played Beethoven's *Für Elise* or Chopin's Waltz in A Minor, her hands fat and clumsy. At twenty-five she was not the graceful woman she thought she would become.

Upstairs hidden underneath her pillow was a postcard from Paris. She hadn't shown anyone the purple ink and spiraling words, becoming smaller and smaller. *L'appel du vide, Call of the void. The desire to do things you know you shouldn't.* Nothing else was written and nothing more was needed. It was a diagnosis of what she had suffered since childhood, the persistent urge for the unknowable, an explanation of why she wanted to poke her fingers through the cage of a fan or smash the dishes and walk across the path of shards on naked feet.

She removed her wedding ring and left it on the lid of the piano. Dilraj began to sing with his awful voice and she followed him, stumbling. She was off rhythm and Dilraj touched her wrist to slow her because she was slipping, she knew it. Halfway through the song, he glanced at her with the same empty look he'd had at the funeral. She had thought it was grief that led them to kiss in the convenience store, their clothes still smelling of seawater and ash, but it was a human-shaped void, and standing at the edge, they had both wanted a closer view.

NALINI COULDN'T CALL it an affair. In Dilraj was Mohinder and in Mohinder was Dilraj. She had read ancient stories where men were married to many wives, and sisters agreed to wed the same man. She could not imagine Draupadi without the five Pandava brothers, all her beloved husbands. And it had happened gradually, no more than leaves darkening for the fall.

Lying naked on the couch, he'd look at her as if he'd known her from another life. Their lovemaking had the familiarity of children who had grown up together, witnessed all the unflattering and lasting effects of puberty. He knew about the troubled tendon in her right arm and the weakness she sometimes felt from it. When he held her, he was cautious not to give her pain, and from this tenderness she felt certainty in how their bodies progressed, each limb entwining in accord. They played cards, three rounds of poker before Dilraj heightened the stakes by asking her what she wasn't willing to lose. Before she could answer, he kissed her, and they both looked surprised at how easily they could move across space, weightless. They could control time too, move years into the past, slow down the future, and pause on the present. As a teenager, she had once found him drunk, passed out in the courtyard, and mumbling through booze-stiffened lips he told her not to tell Mohinder, and she kept quiet, wiped his wet mouth.

Back in Colombo, there was a young entomologist who often visited their home, and as a young girl watching his deliberate and gentle touch as he handled a cricket or a firefly, she longed to transform into something small and frightening that he could cradle in his palm. Love for her possessed a six-legged ugliness to it, and she could still feel the beating of wings, the protrusive eyes. "We're ladybugs fucking," she said to Dilraj before he disappeared inside her. He never spoke of ex-lovers and she never pried too deeply. Although he was a year younger than her, he had dated older girls in high school who had found him reclusive and handsome enough to be intriguing. Whenever she pictured Dilraj, he was always with Mohinder, and she couldn't imagine him alone in the convenience store without his mother or his brother.

The store had been his parents' burden and now it was his. Dilraj showed Nalini the bruise on his arm from a man who had struck him with a Bible. Three days later, a pigeon flew into the store and stayed for a week. He had enough stories like that to hang in a closet. One time many, many years ago a Jewish woman visited the store and asked about his father, who always wore a turban, and he said he was Sikh and she thought he was sick. She told him to get well soon. It was Mohinder's story, but Dilraj sometimes forgot he had heard it secondhand.

Alone, just the two of them, Mohinder was still present. His name breezed into their conversations and lingered between them. When she saw Dilraj's close-lipped smile, it was Mohinder's close-lipped smile. She would hold both their names in her mouth, Dilraj Mohinder, like a single person she had known and loved.

During the daytime, she and Dilraj walked around in nearby parks or watched matinee shows before Arjun finished school. While walking they held hands like they were siblings, lovers, husband and wife. On these outings, she bought small presents for Mohinder, trinkets she thought he might appreciate, which he would later describe as mementos of her treachery. Not thinking of him would have been crueler, his absence complete.

At night she held Mohinder tightly before he removed his suit, waving each article of clothing in surrender of his job, his wasted hours. On the evening of their anniversary he returned home early and Nalini dug into the laundry for a dress and they went out for dinner while Dilraj stayed home with Arjun. Driving through expensive neighborhoods, Mohinder pointed at two-story houses with Greek pillars and expansive balconies as he constructed their future, and on their way home with their breath dreamy with cocktails, everything felt in their reach. They parked down the street from their house and climbed into the backseat like teenagers pulling at each other's clothes in the illicitness of the night, and she thought of her time with Dilraj in the day, their bodies in the sunlight. The reversal made her feel unnaturally whole but wretched, a human with bird wings and a crocodile snout.

She was unsure if she would ever be able to return to being a normal human. "Is there an end in sight?" she asked Dilraj the next day, leaning her head into his shoulder.

He looked up to the sky. "Is the end the beginning or is the beginning the end?"

When the hour arrived to pick up Arjun, they turned to each other, held their gaze like glass.

AT THE END of November, when Mohinder had a day off, they drove as a family to the Cincinnati Zoo. It was cloudy, the air warm and damp, and in the passing wind Nalini still felt brief memories of the summer, when she'd hold the hose high in the sky and Arjun would run around her as they rejoiced in the miracle of water. Mohinder and Dilraj stood by the ticket booth, arguing about who should pay. Mohinder had covered his mouth because he didn't want to make a show of it. They rarely went on outings because of the house, the cost of living, but Dilraj's visit excused indulgence.

Nalini picked Arjun up and twirled him around near the flamingo fence. "Can you fly, mister?" she asked. He nodded and cawed, and she wished this easy affection between them would last, that she could always smooth his cheek and he'd know he was loved.

They first visited the Elephant Reserve, where two Indian elephants enclosed behind a mesh fence moved sluggishly. They had smaller tusks and ears than their African counterparts, Mohinder said, reading the placard out loud to Arjun. When Nalini was a child, she heard of a man being killed after a blessing by a temple elephant, but these elephants looked harmless. They couldn't even be troubled to lift their own trunks. Rabbits thrummed their hind legs with more ferocity.

The tiger exhibit was past the monkey habitat and swan lake, and Arjun roared at each creature. Mohinder was busy staring at a signpost for bonobos when Dilraj lifted Nalini's wrist to check the time. Without turning to him, she pulled away instinctively, not wanting Mohinder to misunderstand. She knew he wouldn't assume anything in a simple touch between family, but he was stressed about work, about a promotion, and lying in bed, where he was more honest, he mentioned things he could not give her, and she wanted to tell him she desired nothing more and was full and content with their lives but when she looked at him, his dark image beside her, she said nothing.

The tigers had pale orange fur but bright eyes, and on seeing the creatures she forgot the glass holding them, imagined the jungles of Malaysia, the sprawl of their bodies in the air after the pounce, mouths opened lovingly to feed. There were no tigers in Sri Lanka.

Dilraj was ahead of her with Mohinder and Arjun. The three of them had wandered into the white tiger zone. Standing by the glass, Arjun pressed his face to the surface and tapped with a fist until Mohinder held his hand still.

"Why are they white?" Arjun asked.

Mohinder squatted and placed one knee to the ground. He gazed over the lanky tiger stretched on the rock, and instead of explaining about recessive genes and how they were expressed when bred with family members, he replied more simply. "It happens with the marriage of two tigers who shouldn't be together."

Arjun opened his mouth wide and then closed it, and the white tiger followed after him, unfurled a soft and deadly paw. The tiger didn't roar but looked straight through the glass and Arjun dropped his arms and took a breath. "Beautiful," he said.

WHEN THE POSTCARDS from Rochelle stopped arriving, Nalini began to feel nervous, but she was not afraid as she had been with her first pregnancy. She felt a warmth inside her spreading, and waking in her body in the mornings was a delight that lasted the whole day, as if she were simply settling down beside a fire. Dilraj had left earlier in the week when a neighbor in Jersey City informed him of water leaking in the store. He packed his things into one duffel bag and drove off the next day. "Who knows how much is lost," he said, speaking to himself, as she imagined he would alone in the store or in the apartment, finding ways to fill the space. She'd see him again on Christmas, and beyond that she didn't bother.

Wedged underneath the lid of the piano was a folded piece of paper she discovered the night after Dilraj left. On the paper was a drawing of two fish on a honeymoon in Fiji with a fake blue ink stamp on the corner. It was unreal, fish walking on land with their exaggerated happiness, popping eyes, too-big smiles, but she kept holding the paper, admiring the patience in his work, the details in the shading, the steadiness of his hand, and she thought of her first love.

Dilraj's mother would have wanted to travel to Fiji to visit her sister. Taped to the cash register in the store were miniature pictures of the country along with magnets, which her husband had bought as a slight consolation for the lives they had led apart. Dilraj's parents had never gone on a honeymoon, and neither had Nalini, pregnant as the moon on her wedding day, Mohinder's mother sobbing through the whole ceremony, telling everyone her daughter-in-law was just very fat. Given the circumstances, they had all lived the best they could manage.

Resting in the nest of her body, Nalini felt herself gaining weight and added the pounds like a new small pleasure. She satisfied her hunger for carrot cake and blueberry muffins, enjoyed eating for two, never having a meal alone. Late at night Mohinder found her eating chocolate-coated waffles, and she said, "I'm preparing for the winter." He kissed her and the way the yellow fluorescence caught his eyes, she wondered if he knew about the baby.

On the evening of his coworker's party, she was bursting in all her dresses, her fat rippling the fabric. She wore coral lipstick and heavy mascara, and finished by clipping her hair to the side so the tips of the strands curled. She rarely put effort into her appearance, and she noticed how Mohinder stared at her as she waited by the doorway. He didn't say anything because he knew those compliments of beauty embarrassed her, made her close her eyes until he stopped. He kept quiet for her sake, and watching him hold his tongue, she wished they placed no restraint on each other and the marriage that joined them could have freed them too.

The Lebowitzes lived in a luxurious seven-bedroom house with high ceilings and a fully furnished patio and pool. A house that could fit another house inside of it. Mohinder toured the place with her and talked with enthusiasm about the crown molding and the chandelier in the foyer, looking hopeful in a way she hadn't seen for a while, and when he kissed her in front of everyone, she was tempted to tell him then, but he looked self-assured, full of his potential, drinking Jack and Coke as he described the paintings Joseph Lebowitz kept of horses and hounds, a series he had purchased in an auction in Philadelphia from a British merchant. They were finely painted acrylic portraits, but the animals possessed subtle smirks and watchful eyes. "Like Mona Lisa," he whispered, close to her ear, reaching with the tip of his tongue. She grinned and Mohinder considered a more serene painting of a baby with wings floating over a pasture.

"Is this also a *Mona Lisa* knockoff?" Nalini asked.

Mohinder tilted forward and examined the painting like a practiced curator. He thought the work was juvenile.

"Dilraj could do better. Remember the watercolors he used to paint inside the store?" Nalini said and paused to inspect a curdle of red and orange.

Mohinder touched the coarse surface of the grassy field spotted with yellow dandelion swirls. "When we were children, Dilraj had a crush on you."

She looked at him, and in his eyes there was no contempt, never contempt.

Mrs. Lebowitz found Nalini in the hallway between the bathroom and the kitchen. She was in her late fifties but moved in the manner of a younger woman and flashed her hips to the sides and punctuated her speech with flourishes of her long fingers. She led Nalini to the kitchen and asked her if she was enjoying herself and offered Nalini a cocktail. "You need to stay warm in the winter," she said and talked about her short-lived stint as an actress in Los Angeles, but her real passion was for the piano, and if she'd had the money back then, she could have been a professional concert pianist. "From what I heard from your husband, you are no stranger to the instrument," she said. "You must play for me sometime."

"I was never that good. Mohinder is too kind," Nalini said, and Mrs. Lebowitz's mouth slackened, her thin lips became even finer, but the woman pressed on to other topics and said, "Drink up, dear. Drink up."

To Mrs. Lebowitz, she finally said, "I'm pregnant," but Mrs. Lebowitz had not heard, already occupied with the laughter percolating through a crowd of women nearby. She excused herself politely, but Nalini wanted her to stay, to reach out and touch her belly.

Across the room, surrounded by his colleagues, Mohinder stared at her while finishing his drink and she did not want his attention. If only she looked more like the other wives, mostly older white women, their faces heavily powdered, concealing what they did not want to show.

EARLY CHRISTMAS MORNING, bundled in a bulky jacket, Nalini's father waited for them on the porch of his new two-story home nestled in a suburb forty minutes outside Jersey City. He had used a decade's worth of savings to buy enough room to fit all his loneliness. "Making my way up," he told her, looking up to the sky, his hair beginning to turn the color of moonlight. From the car, Dilraj carried Arjun, the boy asleep in his arms. In his time away Dilraj had become more taciturn except on the subject of his father, but with Arjun in his arms, Dilraj seemed stronger, made from something more solid than the hasty flint and wood trimmings he appeared to be.

The house was tidy in the style of a bachelor. Her father saved everything, not willing to part with what some people might have considered trash. Near the front door was a Chinese lantern her father's neighbor Mr. Wu had given him last New Year's. It was falling apart, streaks of red paper missing, but the frame was intact, the metal poking out offensively. She wanted to throw it away but her father would notice.

In the corner of the living room, the four-foot plastic Christmas tree, dressed in silver bulbs, teetered to one side. After Arjun woke, they opened gifts and drank cups of hot cider. Her father pressured them all into taking a photograph but managed to leave himself out even after everyone insisted. If Mohinder's mother were around, she would have forced him with a mean grin, her short figure bent forward in disapproval, and one day perhaps such scolding might have softened into love in their old age.

At night Mohinder and Dilraj took Arjun out for a movie, and Nalini sat with her father in the backyard as he drank a beer. He had offered her a can and she declined, remembering all those late nights he had yelled at her for sneaking around because she wanted to be anywhere but home.

"Rabbits live in the yard. I see them squabbling," her father said and squinted into the night. "Mr. Wu complains they eat up his garden."

"You said he's giving music lessons again."

"That's what I hear."

"This house, yours, is too big," Nalini said and looked back at the lit screen door that led to rooms and hallways she had never lived in, and she thought how perfect it would have been for them, her mother and the twins.

The neighborhood was old swampland, so no one kept a basement or buried their dead here. After the rain, the soil was as moist as cake and she wanted to dig her hands into it. "Once you leave Jersey, you don't really come back," Mohinder had told her in the car earlier when they merged onto the New Jersey Turnpike, the night peeling to day.

IN THE MORNING while looking for the toaster in the garage she found old velvet curtains her father still kept. As children she and Rochelle would drape the fabric from hips to shoulders in the fashion of a sari too heavy and warm for anyone living below the equator. "We are becoming," Rochelle would say and curve a tinsel wire into a ring and slip it on Nalini's finger.

When she returned inside, her father told her she had a call, and on hearing her friend's voice she wanted to collapse into it, but instead she gripped the phone tightly like a hand as she had during her first pregnancy, sitting with Rochelle in the clinic and deciding to have the baby.

"Merry Day-After-Christmas, love," Rochelle said. "Do you know in Belgium I have eaten every single chocolate in the country?"

"Aren't you going to bring me back any?"

"I have gained fifteen pounds."

"So have I."

Rochelle was quiet.

"I missed your cards," Nalini said, and then Rochelle cried, closed her mouth to smother the sound. She was alone in a cheap hotel in Belgium after discovering Adrian was married, had three daughters who lived in North Carolina. "You were right," Rochelle said. "Always right."

"No, no," Nalini said, feeling her belly tighten. "You did nothing wrong."

"Tell that to his wife."

That evening while Mohinder and Arjun helped her father install new bathroom cabinets, she was lying in Dilraj's bedroom in his parents' apartment in Jersey City. They were both fully clothed but disheveled, with their jeans lowered and her bra unhooked, disguising whatever was left of their lovemaking, as if there were any reason to hide. Propping his head up, Dilraj told her how his father closed the store on special occasions and they all played rummy, cheating and swindling their way to sweet riches, the colored M&M's they used to bet.

On the nightstand was a picture of his father standing next to his mother. They both posed for the camera, looking neither happy nor unhappy. Nalini had not realized how closely Dilraj resembled his father, from his jawline to the bump in his nose, a likeness that must have disoriented his mother. While the woman managed the store entirely after her husband's death, she begrudged him the fact of his dying. Nalini would overhear her speaking to the magnets on the cash register: *Why do you go driving on icy roads in the middle of the night? Did you buy such a crappy car because you wanted to die? Why couldn't you have brought us someplace warm?* Her voice drained of disappointment, she spoke of all her husband's faults with an encompassing fondness, as if her love was more complete in his passing than in their life together.

"Anything can change in a day," Dilraj said as he pulled Nalini closer, and she felt the crack of his shoulder blades like the sound of doors unhinging. She bit him on the neck and wondered if they could break clean from their bodies.

He sat on his knees and rolled the heel of her foot in his palm. "It will be the year of the rat."

"I'm pregnant."

He held her foot still. "Is it mine?"

Before he could control himself, she heard the panic in his voice, then the shudder of his face, and she dimly shook her head.

He buried himself in her hair, and she stared up at the ceiling, remembered how before her wedding his mother had joked with her, asked if she had chosen the right son.

Nalini waited until she heard Dilraj turn on the shower before she went to the kitchen and checked the fridge and then the bare cabinets. She ate raw, stale handfuls of cereal. It was easier to say the truth that might have been possible. She might have loved Mohinder more, the child might mostly be his, yet she could not help but notice Dilraj had not asked her whether she wanted the child or how she felt, as he had during her first pregnancy. He did not take her hand and draw on her palm with an ink pen. He did not fold her fingers into a fist and cover it with his own.

Sitting in the apartment, surrounded with photographs of the dead, she wanted to remove any trace of herself. She could feel the dryness of her skin, her hands flaking. Turning into a husk of a mother, she thought before resting her head on the table. But after a few breaths her blood quickened and she shot up. Alert with a metallic taste in her mouth, she touched her belly, heard the sound of her own heart beating back.

IN KENTUCKY, SHE kept dreaming of him, and on every occasion, he was alone in the convenience store. She tried fixing her gaze to the postcards before she slept, hoping for mountains, cobblestone roads to seep into her, but she couldn't transport him from the store or find a way inside. Even in her dreams, being together was unimaginable. Instead each night she watched him stand at the cash register as he listened to the vibrations of the washing machines from the Laundromat next door, which sounded like the ocean. He slept better in the store than in the apartment and some evenings he crouched inside the storage closet with a pillow and a blanket, the machines rocking him to sleep, quarter after quarter. When he couldn't sleep, he opened up early, organized the shelves, reviewed inventory.

Like the doctor his parents had always wanted him to become, he distributed quick and easy relief, cigarettes and lotto tickets. He had once given Nalini a slip of paper with a combination of their birthdays. "Do you think we will win?" he asked her, and she tucked it into her warm pocket. Just wait.

IN THE EVENINGS Mohinder rubbed Nalini's feet with lavender lotion. He had told her not to strain herself because of the baby, but she had walked a mile outside in the cold for the fresh air and the grazes of sunlight. She was fattening up, and the weight gave her the satisfaction of undoing herself. "I can see myself in your eyes and I look ugly," she said, and Mohinder shook his head and pleaded with her because she was being cruel. She felt contrite then and punished herself by thinking of their happiness. Later, sitting in a plastic chair in the backyard, she thought of the day, years and years ago, when they had walked by the Raritan River. He was fifteen with braces and spoke to himself in a low, hesitant hum. He was strange, stranger for taking interest in her. Throughout the walk he was watchful that his pace did not exceed hers and in his preoccupation to impress her, he hadn't noticed the rain. They took cover under a bridge, the archway sprayed brightly in graffiti with names of boys, girls, half-written messages. How depressing, she thought, to write one's hopes in such a sunless place.

The stench of mildew and iron slowed her breath, and she covered her nose until disgust gave way to memory, her mother writing poems on the back of used envelopes before tossing them out. She'd find them torn with colorful stamps of birds in the corners and alone in her room she'd try to piece together her mother's words on love, sadness, beauty left to rot with all the morning rubbish. Beside her Mohinder studied the water and she watched him sway in an uneasy rhythm. She accompanied him on a stroll because Rochelle had convinced her, and he had asked her plainly, resigned almost, with no expectations.

He was concentrating on a figure walking in the distance. "If I were you," he said, "I would never fish in this river. They pull out bodies and three-eyed creatures."

"My father is always buying fish frozen from the grocery."

He didn't look at her, but later she heard him repeat the word *always.*

He told her how he had made the walk a couple of times a month for the past three years. He had seen some bizarre things, a man running naked holding a tent as a kite, two women performing a séance as they cried into the water, but it had never rained and somehow this simple cycle of nature seemed more peculiar to him than anything he had seen. "It's a blessing," he said as a flock of geese flew low and skimmed the river, the tips of their wings christened in unholy water.

She hadn't thought much of that day and didn't think she would hold on to it as she had. The memory disappointed her because she had expected more from it, the purposeful movement of the river and the geese, for his words to reveal what she had not seen, that under the bridge surrounded by the blessing of water, she would find forgiveness in the beginning, where nothing was needed, only them.

It would be weeks before they learned of Dilraj's death, how he was found outside lying on a curb of ice, his face turned away from the store. Anything can happen in a day, she heard him telling her. After then there were no secrets between her and

Mohinder, no feeling of hate or envy or love to hide behind. They each grieved privately, unable to look at the other without more agony. For an instant when they kissed, their mouths closed before they could curse. On a Friday morning, three weeks after his death, she woke to find her piano rolled into the front yard, and Mohinder beside it with a hammer, smashing each key with a torturer's precision, waiting for her, for the child wailing inside her, for the whole neighborhood to wake up to their disgrace.

SHADE

MY GRANDFATHER LEANS OUT OF the pickup truck, his bald head slick with sweat, and sings to the traffic on the Garden State Parkway. He's a skinny man but when he hollers in Tamil, he has the voice of a boxer, arms pumped, ready for a fight.

It's July and the heat is on the rise. We're headed to the shore. The beach is only a forty-minute drive from my grandfather's house, but we've been parked on the highway for an hour, the hot air leaking into the truck. My grandfather has removed his green Hawaiian shirt and his shorts. He has a scar from when he was younger and broke his mother's teakettle, the mark spreading from his belly button like tentacles. It reminds me of the days earlier in the summer when we watched television, so lazy from the heat that we sat in our boxers and I'd cool myself with my grandfather's beer, pressing the bottle to my face and licking the sour edge when he wasn't looking.

He coughs and spits yellow phlegm onto the road. His neck is bent and his fingers tremble on the steering wheel, and I know he wants a cigarette.

"You shouldn't be singing," I tell him.

He grins. "Arjun, I still have one lung."

He used to be a fierce smoker. When I was younger, he would smoke a whole pack sitting outside on the porch until the evening light simmered and his breath smelled of ash. My mother told me to keep him from smoking again. But this morning I found an Altoids tin filled with cigarettes by his bed stand. He had been secretly smoking all these days, hiding his habit with breath mints. I kept the tin in my pocket and told no one.

Next to us is a yellow Honda Civic with two girls. Their windows are closed, and I imagine the air-conditioning turning their skin into goose pimples. The girl on the driver's side checks her face in the mirror. When she looks up at me, I slump down into my seat until I disappear under the window.

The traffic starts to move, and my grandfather leans toward me and taps my cheek with his hand. "You know, *little one*," he says, "the heat is an illusion."

I push his hand away, but he tells me about his friend Selvakumar who worked on a tea plantation in Sri Lanka and picked tea leaves from daybreak to dusk. "Do you know how heavy a leaf is," he asks me, "when it carries the weight of the sun?"

I look out the window, trying to find the car with the girls.

As we drive, my grandfather keeps staring at his palm like it's a single tea leaf.

WHEN WE REACH Seaside, my grandfather stops for gas, and I visit the convenience store to use the restroom. I don't really need the toilet; what I want is some air-conditioning.

Walking into that store I feel what my mother must experience each time she enters a temple. My body melts away, and I'm only a being of coolness. An old man with a fisherman's hat procrastinates between two fridges filled with brands of water, while a white, pimple-faced teenager at the cash register stares blankly at the clock. The teenage boy wears only beach shorts. His face is red, and the string of shells on his neck seems to choke him.

I fish into my pockets for money I know I don't have. I walk up to the boy and point at the blue cooler next to him. "Ice, please," I say.

He looks at me. "What, kid?"

"Ice, ice," I say weakly, hand outstretched.

He opens the lid of the cooler, and I see the fresh beer cans, silver and wet. "Here," he says and drops three ice cubes into my palm. I place two in my mouth, and the last I hold in my fist. "Oh man," he says, "you're going to get a brain freeze."

I look up at him.

"What else you want?"

I stand there, unable to speak, my face numb and full. I felt like this once when a girl stuck her tongue into my mouth. She was a year older with a constellation of moles on her cheek, her face chubby as a plum. We were neighbors for a year and a half before she moved to Florida. One afternoon, we were riding bikes at the creek by our school, passing honeysuckles along the way. I dared her to eat a flower. She didn't notice there was an ant in it, but when I told her, she was mad and grabbed my arms, wanted me to taste the bug. She stopped when I couldn't breathe, and then looked at me and said, "You know you're weird-looking. Like your face is all screwed up like a sloth." Then she paused and said, "That's too bad."

From outside, my grandfather honks the horn.

WE PARK AT a meter on the side of the street. My grandfather searches his pockets for quarters.

"When do we need to return to your house?" I ask.

My grandfather wipes his forehead and shows me the six quarters he has found. "One and a half hours."

Sometimes I think we tire my grandfather. He wakes in his own house every morning to our presence. His belongings never stay where he put them last. He blames us and we keep quiet, thinking it is his mind, his memory that he's losing. Years of living alone didn't ready him for our arrival, for my pregnant mother or me, already five then and as tall as her hips, standing by our car overstuffed with our lives from Kentucky.

My grandfather touches my shoulder and points to the boardwalk. From where we stand, the wooden coaster looms over the shore like an old sea serpent. Beside the coaster is a merry-go-round with horses, the paint chipped, the horses' eyes blind with age. His hand is still on my shoulder, and I walk slowly, his weight balanced against me. He gets pain sometimes in his right leg. He doesn't mention it but I can tell.

"I'm feeling tired," I say and sit on the bench bordering the parking lot. He sits beside me, and after a few minutes, I tell him I feel better, and he nods and blames my father, saying he never had good stamina. Before I can correct him and tell him he's thinking of my little brother, he rubs the back of his head and then leans closer to me. "*They say the ogress called misfortune lurks in laziness*," he says.

The line is from Thirukkural, old Tamil poetry my grandfather is always reciting, especially when my brother and I are watching television. "If you memorize the words," he once said, "then no one can take them from you." He also told us about the statue of the poet Thiruvalluvar, at the tip of Tamil Nadu, that is almost as tall as the Statue of Liberty. At school we had started reading poetry by Emily Dickinson, and I couldn't imagine anyone in America making a statue of her that big for her small poems.

The poetry my grandfather recites never interests me, but I repeat after him, not understanding what I'm saying. Now, the only word that sticks is *misfortune*, and I keep hearing it even when my grandfather holds my shoulder and says, "Let's go."

THE BOARDWALK IS crowded this afternoon. I stand by the railing and admire the shore below. Bodies ripen in the sand, and the ocean spreads out and calls with each wave. I am not fond of Jersey water or the many times I have mistaken a plastic bag for a sea creature. But the water today looks cool and welcoming.

"Too many people here," my grandfather says. "No good." He pauses and shakes his head. "My beaches are never like this."

I know he means Sri Lanka and I ask, "How are they?"

"Good," he says. "Not like this."

We walk farther down the boardwalk. My grandfather wants to buy a beer, and I tell him he shouldn't, and he chuckles. "Beer doesn't affect my lungs," he says. "Lung."

Two weeks ago, on my mother's birthday, he was so drunk that he punched the bird feeder I had built. "The quality is poor," he told me, showing his fist full of splinters as proof of my failure. That night I picked each wooden sliver with a boiled needle, while he drank glasses of Johnnie Walker to numb the pain.

He buys himself a Heineken and a Coke for me. He hands them to me but I drop his glass bottle. The vendor says, "Hold still." He comes around with a broom but returns behind the counter to search for a dustpan.

"Making me work even on holiday," my grandfather says, then grips the broom and starts to gather the pieces into a neat pile. I try to stop him, tell him it's not his job to do this, but he continues to sweep and pushes aside all my words.

He is a janitor at my middle school. If I see him wheeling his yellow bin, his mop in one hand, I quickly turn into another hallway. After a boy vomited in my classroom, my grandfather arrived, ready to clean. He didn't look at me. "Thanks, Matthew," my teacher said as he left. My grandfather grinned, and there was a laugh behind his teeth. His name is Muthu.

When we walk farther down the boardwalk, girls pass us wearing bikini tops, their feet naked in flip-flops. One girl in an algae green swimsuit stands by the railing and lifts a polished conch shell key chain to the sun. The light warms her face. She ties back her wet hair, the sea salt dry on her skin, and I can smell the ocean on her. She flips her eyes at me, and I look down at my soda.

Near us, a child grabs her mother's dress and screams for a panda bear hanging from a stall. The woman keeps walking, her eyes ahead, even when her daughter stops in the middle of the boardwalk, points behind her, and cries in long unbroken breaths.

"Ungrateful," my grandfather says and grunts.

He lets me buy a funnel cake, and we sit on a bench, where the seagulls have settled. Sweat threads along his neck and he presses my soda to his head.

"Do you think you will ever go back to Sri Lanka?" I ask. It's something I wanted to ask for a while, but it comes out all wrong because I meant to say *we*.

He snorts. "I only travel in here." He taps his skull.

My grandfather sets a clock nine and a half hours ahead, so when he falls asleep, he drifts across the ocean and starts his day in Colombo. He doesn't talk much about his life in Sri Lanka before the war, only after, as if 1983 when everything ended for some Tamils is when his life began. He reads articles online and stays up talking to other Tamil refugees. I know all about the Tigers with their cyanide capsules and the white vans that kidnap people off the streets of Jaffna. When my grandfather described how soldiers murdered a whole Tamil family in Batticaloa while they slept, my mother told him I was too young to hear such things. "Boys as young as him are fighting in this struggle," he said. "The least he could do is hear what is happening." Last year during the cease-fire, my mother asked him if we could make a trip back, and he looked at her like he might kill her.

There is another Sri Lankan kid in my class, David. But he's a Burgher with Dutch ancestry, blue-eyed and so white he turns red on touch. The girls love him. After a trip to Sri Lanka with his parents, he brought back pictures to show the class. In one picture, a lady hung her child's clothing from a banyan tree, and the wind carved the shape of a body into the fabric. Tanya raised her hand and said the pictures looked gorgeous, and I couldn't deny it. But I didn't see any of the Sri Lanka my grandfather spoke of. My grandfather had once lied and told me there were Komodo dragons on the island. One lick from the creatures, and you're dead. When I asked David about them, he laughed. What island are you talking about? Atlantis?

I toss pieces of funnel cake at the birds and watch how they fight and gobble for the crumbs.

"I want to see Sri Lanka," I say, my voice low.

"Nothing to see," he says and stands and tosses the drink in the garbage. I think of my grandfather's house in Colombo with the grand verandah and the winding staircase my mother described. It was burned down during the riots—along with everything we loved, my mother told me.

LATER MY GRANDFATHER and I go to an arcade attached to a diner. On-screen, I watch a boy drive a red Ferrari into incoming traffic. The car bursts into flames and when he plays again, he dies with the same fury. A waitress asks me if my father is doing okay and points at my grandfather, who sits bent over a table with his head in his hands.

I nod.

"Because if he needs an aspirin," she says, "you just let me know. This heat can make your head go funny." She wears bright pink lipstick, her cheeks full and red as if fresh out of the oven. Her name tag says *Sally*.

My grandfather wants some coffee before we head to the beach. He is tired. I sit beside him as he pours cream and two teaspoons of sugar into his cup.

"Show me your hand," he says.

I open my hand, still sticky from my soda.

"These two lines," he says and touches the tips of my fingers, "mean you have a healing touch."

"Healing touch," I repeat.

"It means you'll make a good doctor."

I don't remind him of the report cards filled with Bs and Cs I have made him sign off on. Or how he dropped me at home when I fainted at the sight of a classmate's mouth filling with blood after he ran into a basketball pole.

"Let me see your hands," I ask.

He doesn't move so I open his closed hand, peeling each finger like a petal.

"You have them too."

He nods like he hadn't noticed.

"Ammappa, maybe you should be a doctor."

He closes his hand. "No, no," he says. "I fix chairs, plug leaks, a different kind of healing."

He has worked as a janitor for nearly twenty years. I saw him hammer a nail into his thumb and continue working until he finished hanging a series of portraits on the auditorium wall as he clutched a bloody napkin. He didn't even tend to the wound until my mother, a nurse, saw his thumb during dinner and raced him to the hospital. I can still see the marks from the stitches near his cuticle.

ON THE BOARDWALK, I see the girl in the green suit again. She sits on a stool and waits for a churro. Her ponytail sways from side to side, swinging to the beat of my heart: Ar-Jun-Ar-Jun.

When we reach the opening for the beach, a poster displays the costs for entering, ten dollars for adults, five for children, and my grandfather shakes his head and turns back in the direction of the car. I wonder if he has forgotten how the beach works or if my mother always took care of it so he never noticed.

"Who wants to pay to see the beach?" he says and holds my shoulder like a cane. "When I was a boy, I had a whole coast to myself. I have never paid for a beach."

His words break off like pieces of the sun: they burn through me. I'm angry with him. I remember the nickel and two dimes he had once given me for a tooth. "Not worth much," he had said and tapped on the metal filling. "Cavity lessens the price."

"It's hot, Ammappa," I yell, and feel people on the boardwalk turn, even the girl in the green suit. She reaches over for the boy next to her, her mouth at his ear, her eyes on my grandfather and me. We must look strange moving around like a single being, with his hand against my shoulder, his shadow replacing my own. His head is still turned toward the parking lot, and when I hear him say, "*Ungrateful*," something inside me sags and I start stabbing the air between us, cursing at him. I know the girl and boy must be watching.

"Stop this, Arjun," he says and keeps walking. I turn and run down the boardwalk and push through the crowd. I don't think he'll follow me, especially with his bad leg, but halfway through the boardwalk, I stop and lean on the metal railing separating the beach from everything else and look back.

The heat is killing me, so I take off my shirt and tie it around my arm into a bandage, picturing myself as a fighter injured in battle and dying, and my grandfather stumbling across my corpse that's too hot even to touch.

Next to me a seagull shakes its feathers and screeches. Before I can even tell it to shut up, the bird flies down to the shore.

The beach is only a six-foot drop from a bed of flat rocks that lie beneath the boardwalk, and looking around, I make my decision quick. Before anyone passes, I jump over the railing. My hands get scraped from gripping the rocks.

I wait for someone to stop me, but no one comes. I stroll past bodies that up close look fried orange and hot, and I stand where the water hits the shore. A wave pushes forward, the trash in the wet sand lying still and breathless.

A boy wearing oversized sunglasses pushes in front of me along with a group of kids, all around the age of my little brother. They squat and hold their knees, letting the water wash over them. When the wave reaches me, it's warm as piss. Somehow this is worse, because now my grandfather is right. This trip hasn't been worth it.

When the boy stands up and spits, his face is bare and his eyes flit across the water, squinting against the sunlight. I can see the fear brighten and finally grip his face when a man with his chest crawling with hair calls out to him in a language I don't understand. They both share the same vaselike body shape.

The only photograph I have seen of my grandfather as a young man is a black-and-white snapshot of him somewhere along the coast of Sri Lanka. He is barefoot, holding a fish almost a third of his size. I was disappointed to see he looked nothing like me. But mostly I wanted to see myself in another place, where I knew the water would be clear and cool, and if I looked down, I would see my toes. I know it's impossible to miss a place I've never visited.

I walk to the abandoned side of the rock hill and take out the Altoids container. I pick up a slender cigarette, place it between my teeth, and light the end the way my grandfather does. Immediately I cough into the sand, ash sprinkling. My chest burns, but I smoke that cigarette to the tips of my fingers until I can no longer breathe, until I know what fire tastes like.

WHEN I RETURN to my grandfather's truck, he is sitting nearby under a tree, facing the ocean he can't see, the view hidden behind a sand dune. I sit beside him, smelling of smoke.

We listen to the churn of water moving closer and closer. He mentions his friend Selvakumar again. How the British had brought Selvakumar's great-grandfather from southern India to work the plantations of Ceylon, to soak tea leaves with his sweat and blood. When independence arrived, it was not a beginning but an end. "They said Selvakumar was not Sri Lankan," my grandfather says. "He had to leave." He speaks of an injustice preserved in his memory like all those lines of poetry he can't forget. I look at him, the awful shape of his bitterness.

My grandfather begins to sing again but quietly. *Desire is like a wave and we're all riding it.*

I answer him by singing along. Stretch the words to carry everything I can't say; pushing endlessly to a distant shore, where he waits, where I would find him.

We sit in that shade long past when the meter expires and the beach has emptied.

AT THE BIRTHPLACE OF SOUND

YOU ARE A CONVENIENCE STORE OWNER, a taxi driver, a doctor, a terrorist, an IT worker, an exchange student. An Egyptian, a Pakistani, a Trinidadian, an Indian. You wear your skin like it's something borrowed, not owned. Like all those hand-me-downs your mother saved that belonged to your brother, so you were always five years behind the latest trends. Who you are right now is temporary, you tell yourself when you break out with acne and miss an audition. You are careless with your mouth and say things you shouldn't say to waiters, to pedestrians, pretend you are tougher than you really are. The fact that you're an actor makes your off-screen bullshit feel natural.

You are thirty but can pass for someone seven years younger. Occasionally, you try out for movies and sitcoms about high school and college students, where everyone is in their twenties, unblemished, past awkwardness, fitting into each other's bodies with ease. Your brother thinks you're an idiot. He'll never tell you this exactly, but he's a lawyer for a big pharmaceutical company and lives with his wife and daughter in a six-bedroom house with brick walls and purple hydrangeas and a half doughnut of pavement, so he never has to back out. You're not jealous because he lives in Jersey, the armpit of America, while you're in Manhattan. The cheap three-bedroom apartment you share with two roommates in Washington Heights is still Manhattan.

When Arjun calls you for dinner, you think of the distance you must travel, the twenty-five-minute ride on the subway and then the hour on the NJ Transit. But when he says, "Karna, Anita wants to see her uncle," you cave in because you imagine your niece's small face looking up with her deep wishbone smile.

You lug a black knapsack and a grocery bag with what you cannot fit. You rarely make this journey out to Jersey, so when you do, you usually stay for the weekend, visit your mother if she's around.

Your brother's wife, Elaine, picks you up at the train station. She waves from a silver Mercedes, her body slight against the wide leather seat. Her dark blonde hair is cut to her chin and hangs like a lampshade. When you sit beside her, she plucks out a pair of used socks from your plastic bag, and you can't tell if she is disappointed or entertained.

"We saw your last movie," she says and reverses the car. "You were spectacular, really something."

"Thank you," you say and don't go on to tell her how those

five lines in the movie, all together fifteen seconds, were probably the highlight of your career. She means well. She is wearing a modest purple blouse that puffs up at her shoulders and a slate gray skirt that reaches her knees. She has a plain face but a kind smile, and when she turns to you and says, "How's Vladimir," your hurt is delayed, and you shake your head up and down like you are watching a champion trampoline jumper. "Good, good. He's all better now."

You keep on smiling as she runs a red light and cuts off someone in the left lane. Cars honk behind you, but you are thinking of Vlad. On your birthday, two months earlier, he ate shrimp for the first time, and his face swelled up to the size of the orange balloon Anita had brought with her. You spent the rest of the evening with your brother and Elaine at the hospital while your mother stayed with Anita at the apartment. No one asked about your relationship with Vlad. You showed no reaction then or later when you discovered him cheating, and somehow you think this makes it better that you didn't lose too much.

THE WOMAN'S NAME is Luz, short for Lucy. She is an eighth-grade algebra teacher at the middle school where Elaine works. She doesn't like cats, Elaine tells you when you don't respond and search the glove compartment for a stick of gum, and you find a map to Niagara Falls.

"She's thirty-seven, but she's never been married."

Elaine knows you also see men, but she thinks you'll come around with the right woman. Two years ago, you were dating a girl named Mei who had her hair buzzed on the sides and a skunk stripe down the center of her scalp. Her body was model skinny, chest flat as a washboard. Elaine still asks you about Mei, tells you that girl had the voice of an angel.

Elaine and your brother met in college during their sophomore year. She was your brother's first girlfriend, and the wonders of the female body awoke in him such fits of longing that when he returned home from college, he spoke with a new passion for his studies. They dated for six years, but you only met her the summer before they got married. You remember her standing on the driveway in a gauzy, ruffled dress, her blonde hair dyed strawberry, her hand tucked into Arjun's. He converted to Christianity to make it easier for her and for her family, who lived in the wilderness of Nebraska. Your mother, a devout Hindu, told him he could be a Hindu and a Christian, said that back in Colombo her neighborhood had a church right beside a temple, that she could hear church bells from her bedroom window.

Your brother is five years older and he thinks this gives him authority over all subjects, including poetry, as when you tried for a year to scrape together bare lines on paper and then onstage, which he remarked was a paltry imitation of William Carlos Williams. Since Arjun was ten, he has had dark fragments of hoofprints under his eyes, the trampled and irritable look of someone being perpetually disturbed. He once told you that you were throwing away your life. "Why would you want an occupation where you will always be waiting?" he said. "Waiting for someone to write a role for you, waiting for someone to think you're important." Looking at him, you felt something inside you split into two and then again, smaller.

WHEN YOU FIRST see Luz, she is sitting in the living room on her knees in a sleeveless dress with Anita beside her rolling a Lego car across her naked, tanned shoulders.

Your brother doesn't fuss over your arrival. He greets you with a request to clean the grill in the yard, and you then wish he had moved to California, wonder why he insisted on staying close to your mother.

He doesn't introduce you to Luz, and you understand he

wants to show you he's not involved in the setup, that he didn't want to call you over for dinner in the first place.

After you wash the metal rack and place new charcoal on the grill, your brother asks you to take out the cat litter. "Rasheed, get out of there," he calls into the dark nook of a hedge. The cat leaps to a patio chair and then to the table and finally claws into your arms. The sudden rush of fur, the scratch marks, the wetness of his tongue make you falter. You want to laugh at the cruelty or irony of holding the cat named after your childhood crush, which you realize you still have not fully grown out of, as if that was the goal, maturing and feeling less.

When you return inside, your niece climbs onto your back and screams, "No more baths," as you whistle like a steamboat. She wears these glow-in-the-dark beads around her wrists, which she holds to your eyes, covering them with her palm, so the fluorescence brushes up against your skin. Luz sits on the couch, and you sense her watching you.

"Prince Karna, Luz is very, very pretty," Anita says, and for a moment, she has transformed into her mother.

"Are you a prince?" Luz asks, and before you can answer, Anita is talking, her feet kicking against your chest. "He's Prince Karna, and my father is Prince Arjuna. In the story, they are brothers, but they don't know it. They are half men, half gods."

You are surprised she remembers the *Mahabharata*, the stories you smuggled into the house as Elaine took her to Sunday school.

"Is that why you're in the movies?"

You crouch down as Anita slides off your back and you ask, "Do you recognize me?"

Luz drums two fingers over her mouth. She has a square face with sharp features that makes her look striking rather than pretty. When she thinks, her forehead bunches into ridges and lines push under her careful makeup. She rotates her foot in a circle, and you notice her legs, smooth as soap. In eleventh grade, your prom date spread her legs in her father's station wagon. Her chiffon dress covered you like a tablecloth, and you smelled her and you laughed. She was a round girl, never dated anyone before you, and she laughed too, matching you because of uncertainty, because she didn't know better, and you needed her giggling as you shoved a pinkie in her and she bled.

"You know you don't look anything like your brother," Luz says, and Anita sticks her tongue out at her and flies out of the room, flapping her arms, onto the patio, where Elaine stands by Arjun as he flips patties and drinks a Corona. Through the window, you see Elaine take a sip from his drink and kiss him on his chin.

"It's strange how we turn out," you say and tell her about the girl in South Africa who was born to white parents during apartheid but appeared black.

She tells you that she's a quarter Mexican. "My grandmother's last name is Cortez. She didn't teach my mother any Spanish because she thought it would get her into trouble."

"That's a shame."

She looks at you closely, leans toward you, presses her index finger along the rim of your chin. "You were that taxi driver in that movie with the hostages."

You smile, bow your head.

ELAINE BLUSHES WHEN she tells you to take Luz with you to the supermarket to buy more burger buns. She's tipsy and holds her beer to her head like she has a fever. A diamond of red skin blazes on her collarbone under a pendant of the cross.

"You can take Arjun's car. It has more gas."

In the car, Luz throws her head back and laughs. "I have never seen Elaine that drunk." She pushes off her wedged heels with her toes and wraps her arms around her knees. "You know

Elaine once gave me a jacket during Parents' Day because she said I looked cold. Imagine that, and she's younger than me."

"How long have you been teaching?"

She pretends to count her fingers. "Ten, fifteen years. Who knows?" She shrugs and looks at a billboard of two girls bending over a used car, asses stamped with dollar signs. "I like it, though, for the kids," she says and then grins, pokes you in the shoulder. "You know you're too young for me."

She brushes her hair to the side, and you notice the tattoo on her shoulder blade. The letters curvy, dressed in black. "French," she says and wipes at it. "That was a mistake."

You have four tattoos. You got your first with your roommate Jason. Your Chinese zodiac sign on your hip, a dragon, or so you thought. It's really the rat, but you say you're a dragon in disguise, a professional shape-shifter. On the back of your ankle you have a star, and on your lower back, you have a snake eating its own tail. A miniature beanstalk winds up your thigh. When Vlad first saw you naked, he touched each ink mark, rubbed the skin, and under his hands, they felt crude, childish, like cartoon drawings.

Luz reaches over for your free hand, places your palm in her lap, and tries to read your future. Her nail cuts your palm into sections. "You'll have a long life," she says, "but you'll have something tragic happen. See how these two lines cross. And your wealth line is short but curves upward, so there's potential."

"Is there any good news?"

She looks closer at your hand, but she just holds it, doesn't move.

YOU WANTED TO become an actor before you even knew it was an occupation. Outside, hanging with other kids in the neighborhood, you played every character: Darth Vader, Wile E. Coyote,

Two-Face. In third grade, while you waited in the hallway, your teacher told your mother that you were too quiet in class, and your mother said the world would be better off if people learned to talk less, and the room was so quiet after she spoke that you heard the sound of your mother's heels tapping against the linoleum floor.

The first time your grandfather told you the *Mahabharata*, you felt yourself slipping into the golden armor of your skin. The son of the Sun God. When your father visited from Connecticut, you kept this ancient secret of your birth hidden. At age nine, you were assigned to draw a family portrait, and you drew yourself, your brother, your grandfather, your mother, and the sun dressed in a suit. Your classmates asked, "Why is your father's head on fire? What's wrong with him?"

When your agent asks—"Can you be . . . ?"—you think of possibilities, of your essence like liquid.

Three months before your grandfather died, he caught you in front of the bathroom mirror imitating his heavy accent, the way he stretched wrong syllables, shortened right ones. He didn't say anything, and you never mentioned it.

Some days on set, when you are playing a part, a taxi driver, a convenience store owner, you hear him trembling behind your vocal cords.

LUZ WALKS UP and down the produce aisle, stepping carefully on only the black tiles.

"The white ones are albino alligators," she says, and you think of Anita sitting on the swing set refusing to touch the grass for fear of sharks.

You pick up a couple of limes for the Coronas in your brother's fridge and catch up with Luz. When you reach her, a young couple passes you. The boy wears a lumberjack hat, and the girl is in a bathing suit covered by a long shirt. She leans into his chest, and her low V neckline reveals pale wedges of her breasts.

The boy blows on the fridge door for the ice cream and draws a heart on his breath. "Buttercup, do you want chocolate or vanilla?" he asks. His hand like a starfish against her striped bottom.

Luz squeezes your hand and looks thoughtfully at bags of SunChips on sale. "Pumpkin, what else do we need?"

You slip into the role easily and swing your arms around her waist. She kisses you on the cheek and the act feels natural. Other customers pass you and Luz, and you imagine they see nothing more than a loving couple, and you wish Vlad were among them walking down the grocery aisle, witnessing the moment of intimacy, and feeling something, if anything, for you still.

ON THE DRIVE back, Luz cracks open the window and turns the radio to a Latin station and hums along. Her voice sounds sad, but she is smiling as you show her your old high school and the street that leads to your childhood home. "It was my grandfather's house," you tell her. "We lived with him all my life. He died when I was fourteen."

You don't stop to visit the house because your mother would not be there. She has flown out to Colorado to visit an old friend, a doctor who used to work at the same hospital as her. When you were young, he visited the house, brought you chocolates and sour candies, and carried you around on his back. One evening, he stopped on the highway to help two stranded passengers and was struck by a truck, lost the use of both his legs. Your mother told you how when the paramedics found him on the roadside, they thought his red hair was blood. Too distraught with grief, she didn't realize she shouldn't be telling you these things.

After the accident, he came to the house only once, looked

hesitantly at you when your eyes wandered to the wheels of his chair, and you wished in that moment you could break your own legs and not have to walk anywhere ever, become part robot. Your mother sat outside with him in the backyard, where the sun hit, and she took his hand and they didn't say a word. You still find it hard to imagine that your mother has a life without you.

Luz says her father owned chickens and used to make eggs a different way each day of the week. She lived with him on the weekends, when the eggs were poached and scrambled. Some days collecting the eggs, she accidentally dropped them and felt a murderous guilt. When she was in college, she needed money and sold two of her own eggs. "Like that," she says, "I might have children running around this world, looking just like me, and I don't even know them." She laughs but it comes out more like an ache. "It's the old mother or egg question. Which comes first?"

You and Luz pass a tall concrete tower with a lightbulb and a shack no larger than a rest station. Luz tells you to slow down as she reads the sign—*Thomas Edison Museum.*

Her eyes brighten. "Let's go inside. Have you been?"

You shake your head, remember how you passed the place your whole life and never had the desire to step inside. You don't want to stop the car, but she has her hand on the door, ready to leave.

THE MUSEUM IS tiny and crowded with inventions, glass-covered relics from Edison's laboratory. You don't walk beside Luz but behind her, wary of your movements. The curator stands by a phonograph that blooms behind his head like a rare brass tropical flower. His glasses rest on the ridge of his nose, and his black hair pulls back to show delicate scalp. He points at a circular pin on his breast pocket and says, "This is young

Thomas Edison," and you think he is dipping into the past to reveal himself to you.

"Please sign the logbook," he says. "Where are you two from?"

Maybe because one of the phonographs is playing a waltz, or because Luz is admiring a miniature model of Edison's laboratory and the curator looks so curious and welcoming, you say, "We're from Philadelphia. We are traveling back home from a convention in New York. We're lawyers."

Before you finish, Luz is standing by your side, staring at you. You're alarmed but you sign the logbook, making up a street address in a place you have never visited.

"Oh, very nice," he says. "The first Philadelphian lawyers we have had yet."

He asks if you have time for a tour and you look down at your watch and notice you have spent almost an hour on this trip to get burger buns. Luz must sense your feelings, and she shakes her head. "We'll just look around. We have to get back soon. Our son is with the babysitter."

You can feel your pulse as you follow her down a narrow corridor. She reads placards from the wall: *In Yawata City, Japan, Thomas Edison is treated like a Shinto god!*

"How does one imagine," she says, "that you could capture sound and even light."

You are wondering what your child would look like with her nose, your mouth. You once saw a Chinese-looking kid with red hair and freckles at the arcade in Chuck E. Cheese's when you were ten, and you remember the excitement you felt when you saw her.

You are half-Punjabi, half–Eelam Tamil. The difference doesn't show on your face. Your parents divorced before you were born, and your mother in her heartsick confusion gave you her last name hyphenated along with your father's, which you shorten from sixteen letters to six for casting callbacks. Vlad likes the sound of your name. He told you this the first time you met him, at an Upper East Side party hosted by an old college classmate named Mario. Vlad wore a Metallica T-shirt under a blazer and drank vodka and cranberry juice out of wineglasses. He had an ease to him that you found charming. By the time you made your way over to talk, he was tipsy. Everyone you talked to that evening was from elsewhere—Brazil, Poland, Argentina, Nigeria—so you were only a little surprised when Vlad spoke in a slight accent and said, "India?"

"No, no," you stumbled. "I was born here. Only half-Indian."

"Pradeep, here, is from India," he said and pressed his hand on the shoulder of a young man who stood by the window and wore an unattractive beige jacket that reminded you of all the aunts and uncles who visited your grandfather's house for birthdays and dinner parties.

You told Pradeep your name, and he began to speak to you in Hindi. When you said you didn't know Hindi, he quieted, embarrassed for you. Right then you wanted to explain yourself to Vlad, tell him about all the languages spoken in India and the unfair dominance of one, but instead of mentioning borders, the shoddy doodles of British cartographers, you take a sip of your gin and tonic.

"I'm surprised," Pradeep said, "they named you after that unlucky prince, the one that keeps giving whatever's asked, the one slayed by his own brother."

Vlad repeated your name as he looked at you. He had a ring of stubble around his mouth and eyelids that drooped. He agreed the name sounded tragic. Later, after a year of dating, when you felt Vlad slipping away, you told him you wanted to adopt a child. You really had no interest in a child, but then over the weeks, the idea took hold of you and one night, you told him, "We can have a surrogate. Mix up our sperms so we don't know."

Still the child would belong to only you or Vlad. He kissed you and said, "Nothing's perfect." But you wanted to belong to him so badly, you pulled yourself closer to him, and tried not to think of what kept you apart, his years at private boarding school, the professional squash games he played, the way he smiled at you when you mistook the sport for a vegetable. He knows five languages, and you know two, both poorly.

Standing among museum relics, you remember the family gatherings, the ten-hour road trips to nowhere, eating lemon-and-curd rice at rest stations, where you called everyone aunty and uncle though they weren't related to you, and their children, whom you saw on a handful of occasions, filled up your birthdays, broke your presents, fought for the icing flowers on your cake, and wished you a happy, happy day—all were parts of a childhood you had not cared for, and now thinking of your son, who would never have to listen to cassettes of bhajans and deal with people he conversed with only in formalities, people who would drop everything to pick you up at an airport, hospital, cook meals when your mother was ill, all because they too traveled that same distance separating one part of the world from the other, you feel as if something dear has perished.

OUTSIDE THE MUSEUM, there is a trail through a swath of forest where Edison's laboratory once stood. As Luz and you walk through the path, you spot two white-tailed rabbits and a sparrow's nest, and with the murmurs of traffic from Route 27 everything feels more alive.

"It's getting late," you say, but Luz is busy imagining the life of the Wizard of Menlo Park. She stands on a tree stump, rubs her chin, and looks up into the sky. "We're at the birthplace of sound," she says.

Her long legs cut through the landscape, rise like new wooden stems. She repeats her name over and over again, and seated on the dry ground, you hear it play back in your head, vibrate with new meaning.

She asks you if you think Thomas Edison sat on the stump when he was tired of the laboratory. "Or maybe this is where he got his inspiration."

Thomas Edison strikes you as foolish. Inside when you read the sign, *Genius is 1 percent inspiration, 99 percent perspiration*, you wanted to laugh as you thought how replaceable genius is with failure in our short, determined lives. And you think you will never pass this stage of existence where you are trying to light a bulb with beard hair and a fishing line and that you'll die with cat fur in your fist. You would be the idiot your brother always knew you to be. When he handed you the keys this afternoon, he told you to drive carefully and you wanted to crash the car.

You have never been close with your brother except when you were young and didn't know better. He once tricked you into eating purple Play-Doh, and you were sick for three days, the chalky taste lingering in your memory. You haven't forgiven him for telling your prom date she was going out with a fag. When you found Vlad with another guy, you took the train to Jersey because when someone screws with your heart, somehow home feels irrevocable. Your brother met you at the coffee shop across from the station, late in the evening. He grabbed you by the neck for an embrace and bought you a coffee, remembered how you like it with two packets of sugar and a quarter cream. He talked about all the shitty work he did that day and didn't ask what was wrong, and you were grateful.

You tried not to read the situation too closely for meaning about your relationship with your brother. Vlad told you it was a problem of yours, overanalyzing the little things that didn't matter. But when you look up at Luz, she bends down to pick up a caterpillar clinging to her toe and places it in your palm, and you think you understand the offering, this small life.

What you want most now is to lose your body, and the way she holds your gaze you know she does too. She doesn't kiss you but holds you, her hands under your shirt, her dress pulled up above her thighs. You lean into her touch and lift her until she's a part of you. Under the afternoon light you close your eyes, imagine layers of yourself giving way until there's only your breath moving back and forth, back and forth.

BROWN SMURF

THE SUMMER MY FATHER ANNOUNCED his engagement, my mother planned a two-week trip to Lake George with Gurmit's family, who owned a vacation home at the lake. They would often visit us in Jersey, where we lived on wetlands with more roadkill than wildlife, and maybe sensing our gloom, they spoke of the beauty of the Adirondack Mountains. "Have you ever felt pure bliss?" Uncle Darshan would ask, his legs outstretched on the table. "It's sitting by the lake and seeing a sunset that looks like a golden veil." Those days my mother pulled extra shifts at the hospital and didn't have the energy to deal with my brother and me and our endless wants. She didn't seem to mind that we never showered, slept in front of the television, and ate from the bowls of our hands. When Gurmit's family arrived, she would sit with a fist under her chin, her eyes closed, like she was listening to her Walkman, Tina Turner singing to her about dreams.

My brother and I spent those evenings eating whatever we pleased. Hershey's chocolate bars and coffee cakes from ShopRite were laid out on the carpet like ritualistic sacrifices. Gurmit looked forward to these visits, his fingers bloated and hungry. He wasn't on a diet but his parents refused to buy him junk. The skin around his waist sagged, and he would lift his belly like it was a dress. He was eleven and wore thick beige framed glasses with black string attached to the corners, so they wouldn't run away from his face. His hair was wrapped in an orange cloth that knotted on the top of his head into a bun. I knew his hair reached the crown of his ass but I had never seen it, and he wouldn't show me. "My hair is for Guru Nanak," he would tell me. I wondered if it was because I wasn't a proper Sikh. My father was Sikh, but he never wore a turban, and I had only been to Hindu temples with my mother, where I would sit with my legs folded and my eyes closed, praying that I wouldn't fall asleep.

Gurmit lived in a small town in Pennsylvania, where the number of cows almost equaled the number of residents.

"This place is all white," Gurmit's mother said when we drove over for lunch one Sunday afternoon. She wore a salwar kameez, her eyelids painted purple and her lips the dark shade of cherries. My mother sat across from her in the living room in an old striped T-shirt, her hair pulled up in her usual style when she was about to clean. She wore no makeup, and her eyes looked swollen like she had been crying.

"Do you know what?" Gurmit's mother continued. "His classmates call him Al."

"Why Al?" my mother said and looked over at me at the dining table reading a book. My brother, Karna, was in Gurmit's room playing video games.

"Short for Al Qaeda. They see the turban, and they think he's a Muslim."

"Baljit, children don't know better and are lazy. When I started high school here, no one knew where Sri Lanka was. I could have been from Jupiter for all they cared."

My mother reached over for Aunty Baljit's hand. They had known each other briefly when we lived in Kentucky before my parents split. Aunty Baljit and Uncle Darshan moved to Delhi before Gurmit was born, and they returned to the United States when he was eight, young enough for him to acquire an American accent.

Aunty Baljit looked at me and then lowered her voice. "Gurmit is such a gentle soul. He sweeps the earthworms from the sidewalk and the driveway after it rains so I don't run over them with my car."

She leaned closer to my mother. "Do you know what else they call him? A Brown Smurf. What is a Smurf?"

We ate dinner in the living room. Aunty Baljit spread out dishes of vegetable curry and pilaf along the dining table, and we served ourselves on paper plates, taking a seat on the couch or on the red Persian rug that covered the living room floor. Uncle Darshan talked about his work in the spice business. He traveled back and forth between the United States and India, and every time he returned with a fresh complaint about his journey. "You know what the real difference is between India and America?" he said, pointing his index finger at us. "There is no rule of law in India. You need to bribe everyone to live a normal life. I give ten rupees each day to a man so he would turn on my water supply. Someone can bribe a judge and that scoundrel can take away your land."

He spoke of India like a mistress he wanted to give up but kept returning to night after night. Even the house was decorated with reminders of the country they had left behind. A copper vase stood in the foyer with peacock feathers. Paintings belonging to the time of Tagore. The metal shelves embossed with imprints of mangoes and palm leaves. My mother had called the house grand like a manor, and out in the rural plains of Pennsylvania she might have been right, but I always left remembering the orderliness of the house, the way everything had a purpose unlike in my grandfather's house, where we all lived in the clutter of what he refused to give up.

Uncle Darshan wore a bright red turban and before he leaned forward to tell us another tale, he drank from his mug, and I pictured him as Papa Smurf and Gurmit seated beside him stuffing his face with smurfberries and sarsaparilla leaves.

MY GRANDFATHER DIDN'T like traveling more than four hours from his house, and Lake George was near the upper border of where he dared to voyage. On the drive upstate, my brother listed facts about Lake George: it was named after King George II and was home to the Loch Ness monster. I told him he needed to check his sources, but he shook his head, certain of himself.

Karna spent so much time caved up in his imagination that he wouldn't even know if he pissed himself. My mom forced me to shoulder him anytime I went to the mall, the movies, or across the street to Rasheed's house. I had just turned fifteen and Karna was ten, all quiet and skinny back then; it was easy to forget about him. Rasheed and I once watched a video where all the ladies were topless. Classy, Rasheed called it, because the girls still had on their underwear. We hadn't noticed my brother, but he was staring intently at the screen, his hands folded on his lap. Rasheed said Karna would start seeing breasts wherever he went, anything round that he could squeeze in his hands.

My brother sat cross-legged in the car playing with my old Power Rangers wristband. He never took it off except once when my mother caught him wearing it into the shower, the weeks of grime a stripe along his skin. From the front seat, my grandfather asked my brother to recite the presidents, and my brother, who had practiced for weeks for his history presentation, started with George Bush, whom he dubbed George II, and went backward, pronouncing each name carefully as if they were loved ones, as if he were leading us through our long ancestry in the country.

My mother asked him to stop when he reached James Garfield. "My head will explode," she said, raising one hand from the wheel. She made a sound with her mouth that reminded me of our vacuum choking on a lost coin. I imitated her, and then Karna did, and we both laughed. My grandfather said he wanted to get out of the car soon.

When we neared Lake George, still on the highway, I saw two balloons tied together in the sky, and the image held me, the shape of breasts, purple and airy, rising to the heavens.

THE SUMMER HOME was lined with Indian paraphernalia in the front yard. Totem poles and wigwams rose from the land. A statue of an Iroquois chief greeted us from the porch. The paint was chipped around his chin and revealed a white ceramic center. "All this came with the house," Aunty Baljit explained. The owners were thrilled at the fact Indians were moving in, told them all the artifacts were free of charge.

I shared a bedroom with Gurmit and Karna. My mother

stayed in the den on a futon while the two remaining bedrooms went to my grandfather and to Aunty Baljit and Uncle Darshan. Back in Jersey, I shared a room with Karna, and I didn't want to spend my vacation crammed up with them, so I told my grandfather I needed my own space. He was changing his shirt before a night stroll through the forest. He looked tired with his head hunched, his fingers working slowly on his buttons.

"We're only here for a short time," he said and patted my arm. He stared at me for a moment before descending the stairs. His reading glasses rested on the nightstand and his shirts hung from the wardrobe. A pair of pants was left tangled and forgotten on his bed. And I just stood there—even years later—feeling his absence.

The room I shared had a queen-sized bed, and we slept head to toe, but with Gurmit there the bed narrowed and the springs jiggled whenever he turned. He wore his hair wrapped to sleep. As an only child, he must not have been accustomed to shared spaces: the unnamable stink, the short supply of air.

I told Gurmit and Karna ghost stories. How the house was built on an Indian burial ground, where women and children were slaughtered by white colonists. "They would eat their eyes," I said, "so they wouldn't come searching for them in the afterlife." I think Gurmit thought the colonists were after him too. Each night, he tied a tinsel-colored cloth over his eyes and kept a baseball bat by his bed. Like he planned to kill piñatas in his sleep, pillage them for candy.

I began to feel sorry for him, but then he started in about his dead aunt. The afternoon my brother was hooked up to his asthma machine, I walked with Gurmit into town for ice cream. He spent fifteen minutes pacing between butterscotch and rocky road, smudging his fingers across the glass case.

"You can have both," I said.

He squinted his eyes and then shook his head. "No, I'll have butterscotch."

We sat by the lakeshore, where women sunbathed on their stomachs with their bikini tops unclasped. The wind swept through us, left us with cravings for crabmeat and open fires. Gurmit had a thin cream mustache and beard patch. He was staring at the women with his lips parted and his glasses tilted forward. I pointed to my face and he rubbed his mouth against his arm and grinned, patting his belly. Even his satisfaction felt pathetic, and I put my arm around him and thought I would help him out. He had no siblings, no one older like Rasheed to watch out for him, to tell him about women and life. I was about to ask him if he had ever seen a naked lady before, but then he closed his eyes and said, "Last night, I had a dream of my mother's dead sister. She took me by the hand and made me breakfast and then we walked in the park, and she pushed me on a swing and we fed the ducks. I was just talking to her, and she listened. I don't know what I said, but it didn't sound like English or Punjabi." He paused and waved his feet from side to side. "It was the best day."

He leaned down, cupped the water in his palms, and drank, sighing between sips. I crouched beside him and asked when was the last time he saw his aunt before her death.

He shrugged. "She died during the 1984 riots in Delhi. I never met her."

RASHEED TOLD ME when you're with a girl you need to lie about your experience, and since I was a virgin, I needed to pretend I had been with at least three girls, and that I needed to use my imagination for the real thing to happen. There was a girl named Yvelis I sometimes hung out with. She had straight hair that reached her shoulders and acne scars on her cheeks.

She whistled through a gap between her front teeth when she spoke. She wasn't pretty, but she let me kiss her on the neck until there was a dark train of sores, and in her basement, I touched her breasts, the television washing over us like plastic moonlight. Another time at one of Rasheed's parties, I was lying on the floor, drunk off pink magic punch, and a girl sat on my face and curtained me in a blue cotton sky of longing. I tried to imagine the girl was Yvelis, but I couldn't and I felt a little bad that it didn't really matter.

I was running track that year. Rasheed had convinced me it was a good way to stay in shape during the winter, but I didn't really care about any of that. Rasheed did it for the girls, and I had nothing better to do. Training was not as exhausting as I expected, and I started to enjoy the feel of my own body pushing against my will. During the trip I planned running routes through town and by the lake. In the mornings I saw the same Frenchwoman sitting with her chihuahua, the leash tied to the bench. She would read the paper and slant her head in my direction whenever I passed. Outside a bakery, the owner always waved. He had first seen me heaving by the store and had offered me a cup of water. The town felt quaint, the high school right across the street from a pizzeria, and it was strange I couldn't imagine living there or anywhere else we passed on our drive up except for my own miserable town.

At midday we swam in the lake when the heat stuck to us like jelly, but we preferred the evenings, when crowds disappeared into restaurants and bars, and only the occasional nightwalker or drunkard came to admire the water and let their voices skip along the lake's surface, and for the most part we had the water to ourselves without the supervision of lifeguards and adults.

My brother had weak lungs and swam poorly, but he wanted to one day swim across the English Channel. The notion struck him after he watched a documentary on Florence May Chadwick. I don't know what about the woman or rough water inspired him and never cared to ask. I tossed it aside like any other random fact my brother told me. Together we swam as far as we could across the lake and breathed in the smell of the fresh water, thankful our eyes didn't burn. Karna never made it far and returned to the shore for rest. He sat on a flat-faced rock and poked his legs into the water while I pushed on until my limbs tired and all I could manage was to float. When I headed back, I'd see him, a shiver against the landscape, and I would hold his image each time I lifted my head to breathe.

"You have to avoid kids like Gurmit," I told Karna after he'd wandered off with Gurmit into the woods to search for newts and tadpoles. "They'll make you look bad. Remember you're not really friends with Gurmit, only family friends. There's a difference."

"What's wrong with Gurmit?"

"He's nice, but truthfully no one likes him, and if you hang around with him, no one will like you either."

Karna didn't answer, and I thought that we understood each other. He was tapping on his Power Rangers wristband with the same two fingers he used to tell where the wind was coming from. He hugged his knees and looked at me. "Do you think Amma is heartbroken?"

"They got a divorce like a decade ago. Time heals everything," I said, repeating what I read from a fortune cookie. When Rasheed put me in a headlock and popped my shoulder, I forgave him twenty minutes after the pain.

"What if he has kids after he gets married?"

"Then we'll have our half-Japanese siblings with their squinty eyes."

"That's not nice."

"The world is not nice, Karna. You have to be prepared. If

you are a kid like Gurmit, people start saying things about you. If you're too quiet, people will think you're some dumb mute."

Downstairs I heard Uncle Darshan and Gurmit preparing to sing Shabad. Their voices climbed up and down the stairs with a range of ragas. Karna looked toward the doorway and was silent.

GURMIT HAD ANOTHER dream about his dead aunt. She was sitting in a rowboat and painting her toenails while he read her a poem.

"Sounds pretty dull," I said and watched a pair of ducks gliding across the lake in the evening darkness. "Aren't ghosts supposed to be more exciting?"

"A man with a machete cut through her. She was sixteen."

"Did she tell you this?"

"I saw the scars on her face and arms."

"Shit, Gurmit."

"I was reciting what your grandfather says. *Death is like sleeping and birth is like waking up from that sleep.*"

"Thirukkural," I said, and thought of my grandfather sitting on the sofa and reading old Tamil poetry as he tried to tell us about life. Somehow in Gurmit's handful of visits, where he was busy snacking on whatever we gave him, he had managed to listen and stuff all those words into his mind. I wasn't angry at Gurmit but felt as though I was about to lose something and I wouldn't even know where to start looking for it.

My brother had swum far into the lake, the farthest he had the whole trip. When he emerged from the water he was trembling, his mouth open and hacking up air. I searched his bag for his inhaler, and when I couldn't find it I told Gurmit to stay put and ran back to the house. As I passed a convenience store, someone cried, "Watch out," but I didn't look back until I was home.

No one seemed to be in the house. Uncle Darshan's car was gone, and when I called out, I heard only the borders of my own voice. By the time I returned to the lake, I was out of breath and Gurmit was beside Karna holding his hand. He pushed the wet hair from my brother's eyes and whispered something I couldn't hear.

The next day my mother stood us in front of her and looked us over. She said she was checking us for ants but really it was for ticks. She had once found one on the back of my brother's arm and kept it in a jar to show the doctor to make sure he didn't have Lyme disease. She was upset with us now for swimming in the dark and for our carelessness, but she didn't say more than "You both know better," before she touched both of our cheeks and asked us if we were hungry.

My grandfather was sitting in a rocking chair snoring, and Uncle Darshan, Aunty Baljit, and Gurmit were out at the grocery store. My mother cooked eggs and warmed toast, and looked happy as she watched us eat. I asked her if she was having a good time at the lake. She brushed my hair with her fingers and said, "Of course." I knew she was glad to be with us and away from Aunty Baljit and Uncle Darshan for a few hours. To comfort my mother, Aunty Baljit made weak jabs at the imaginary woman my father was marrying that neither of them had met. "That woman is not so pretty. Not like you!" or "She must be an awful person to do this to you," speaking to my mother as if her marriage was recently ruined by this woman and had not ended years ago.

My mother must have felt lonesome in their presence when we sat together for a movie in the living room and Uncle Darshan reached for Aunty Baljit's hand, bringing her palm to his lips and blowing before she could pull away, clicking her tongue *Chi* as he laughed. I didn't ask my mother how she felt about my father's marriage or how she herself had come close to getting remarried. When she asked me if I wanted to attend my father's wedding, I said I didn't care and she looked disappointed.

Later that day we sat on the porch and watched the sunset Gurmit's parents were always raving about, and I saw no beauty in it, nothing miraculous in the marmalade color of the sky. My brother eyed a beaver straggling under the house. "I think it's blind," he said.

My mother shielded her eyes. "If it were," she said, "it would be dead already. Nature is not kind in that way."

I FOUND THEM by the lake. It was early evening, not too dark, but still I carried a flashlight as I walked. I didn't see them at first because they were crouched low near a patch of water marigolds wearing their blue and black swim trunks. They were rolling around, not really kissing but licking each other, on the cheeks, on the ears, drifting to the belly button. My brother showed all his teeth like he'd won a prize. They were laughing, and before all the rage, I think I felt jealousy, as if I'd shined my flashlight on them and seen suddenly with such clarity how easy it was for some people to love.

I punched Karna hard on his chest, and he bit his tongue and his mouth bled. In a day, the bruise would shape into a horseshoe, a dark grin, but Karna would wear a T-shirt and show no one, not even our mother, and in exchange I said nothing. That night, Gurmit ate sparingly and left the remains of his chicken and rice, and Aunty Baljit touched his cheek and asked if he was feeling sick. My brother, who finished his meals with an apple, didn't break from his routine. He peeled the skin with his teeth and ate that thin layer before carving into the pale hunk of the fruit, and, watching him, I tasted the sourness.

Sleeping together in the queen bed, I stayed in the middle and lashed out at their restlessness during the night, jabbed them in the ribs, and called them freaks. "The white colonists are going to get you. They killed witches," I said, though I knew the women were all innocent. My brother and Gurmit didn't move, retreated into their sleep.

We only had a couple of days left but I spent most of my time indoors while Karna and Gurmit went down to the lake. They woke early and dressed while the sun was rising, and the images of them rubbing their eyes, grabbing their towels, felt like shreds of dreams when I woke to an empty room. They must have hated me, but when I held Karna's arm, still wet after one of his lake excursions, he didn't break free but stood there looking at the wooden floorboards, and I let him go and kept quiet, as if this was how it would be between us, our senses severed. Still my imagination pushed against me, and I saw their naked bodies entangled in perverse patterns of feet and arms and wished I could cut off that limb of my soul that was him.

My grandfather wasn't especially lively company. He had caught poison oak and mostly stayed in his room. He wore a thick layer of chamomile lotion he scratched through every few hours, which my mother would reapply as she scolded him. While he slept, I searched his room for stray cigarettes I knew he stashed somewhere unseemly—a sock, the toothbrush holder, the bottom of his underwear drawer—where no one would suspect. He sank into a heavy sleep, but the itching woke him in unexpected fits, and on one occasion he discovered me bent on my knees cracking open the flimsy sole of his dress shoe, and I asked him where he kept his chessboard. We played three games, and I lost all of them. My grandfather, eager to point out my weaknesses, mentioned the knight I had left open, the bishop I had failed to manipulate, and I almost slapped the board, but he said I needed to be more mindful and I didn't want to prove him right. He was ready to return home to his own bed, as was my mother to see her patients. The mountains and the lake were all more distractions than any real solace. They looked forward to the normalcy of their days, everything I dreaded and dreamt of. My grandfather had once said the body didn't handle change well, and he might have been right with his skin puckered, the bumps round and transparent like frog eggs.

Uncle Darshan only owned books about Indian cuisine and cricket. I flipped through them when I was bored. One evening Uncle Darshan sat next to me and peered over my shoulder. "I was hoping Gurmit would become more interested in sports," he said, and I knew what he really meant was cricket.

I wanted to tell him Gurmit would love chasing after boys in the summer heat, but instead I said maybe the last and only kind thing for Gurmit, "You never know what the future holds," which I thought sounded wise and reassuring. Uncle Darshan patted my head and went to pray.

I had heard stories of how Uncle Darshan had the best batting average in Gaggomahal. He was more religious than my father and besides telling me cricket stories, he taught me about the soul and the ego and the truth we must seek in our daily lives. Next to him, my father with his cropped hair and plaid shirts looked plain. My father would embrace me lightly with one hand pressed against my back, while Uncle Darshan buried me in his arms so I could smell traces of cologne on his skin and the spearmints he carried in his pockets.

"I wish Uncle Darshan was our father," I had once told my mother when I was younger.

She frowned. "Don't say that. What would your father think?" she said, exasperated in a way that reminded me of the dates she went on, when she would sit by her bedroom mirror applying rouge and lipstick, but always with strict formality as though she found no joy in the process and would rather undress and sit in the tub and wash herself of the day.

• • •

WHAT I REMEMBERED of my father's departure was my brother's arrival, the two events forever linked. I never blamed my brother, but during his early years, when I saw him in his crib, his little hands reaching out for me, he carried all the anger and sadness of my father's absence, and at the edge of the lake, lying around with time, I caught the shape of those old feelings.

The evening before our departure Gurmit started jabbering more passionately about his dead aunt. He described her face and her habits in such vivid detail over dinner that Aunty Baljit broke out in tears. But he couldn't stop, and forgetting his aversion for me, he privately told me how his aunt had fallen in love with the cinema owner's son. They almost ran away and married.

"Quit it," I said.

"Ma told on them and the boy married another girl. It was her fault."

"Aunty Baljit, your mum, is crying about all this."

"Your mum cries too."

I wanted to punch him, but I knew there would be no satisfaction in that, and instead I took the higher road and called him a flubberfag. Gurmit was called so many names that I don't know if what I said even registered, but he was smart and simply ignored me, walked away like I was no more threatening than a sofa.

In the room, Gurmit and my brother packed for their final trip to the lake. They were methodical and moved in the practiced silence of the mornings. Lying on the bed, I watched them, and their eagerness for the night made my own boredom from the past weeks seem immoral. Fat slivers of dewy, sun-flecked minutes thrown away that some kid might have died to taste. Rasheed would have agreed, especially since he believed our purest selves were in water. He once did it with this goose of a girl in the swimming pool and whenever he had a chance, he would remind me of that feeling he had of life just beginning.

After the two left, I combed and gelled my hair, slipped on a button-down shirt that I was told made me look older. I had sprouts of a mustache, nothing like Rasheed's bristly beard and sideburns, which gave the impression of a man in his thirties. I had grown six inches the past year, but still it didn't show in my shoulders or chest. I was all length, paper-thin.

My grandfather was seated on the porch when I left. He was scratching his arms in the privacy of the darkening sky. Hearing my footsteps, he turned from his chair and his face loosened when he saw it was only me. Four years later, when he was dying, I would search for a trace of that glance when I'd lead him outside to revel in the flowers, the bush of tiger lilies that clawed the air and hid the street.

"It's cool outside," he said, and I nodded, pausing next to him. The view in the twilight might have been beautiful, but I didn't have the patience for it.

"I'm going for a run," I said.

He didn't inspect my clothing, simply continued with his scratching. "Tell Karna and Gurmit it's getting dark."

His eyes were just slits of skin. When he turned his head in my direction, I could tell he wasn't looking at me, but I saw him fully.

By the time I reached the bar, it was still early, and I stood near the doorway, tucked my shirt into my pants, and watched couples and groups of men and women pass inside. They were mostly white, and I stayed as still and quiet as the Indian chief statue on our porch. Maybe because I was alone, without Rasheed or anybody, I thought they could see through me. I busied myself by checking my pockets and searching through my wallet. If I had a cigarette I might have felt more at ease, though I was a nervous smoker, always waiting for someone to discover me mid-breath, choking on some half truth.

Across the street was a 7-Eleven and through the window I saw the man behind the register, familiar with his unruly mustache and anxious gaze that reminded me of my grandfather. Back home at liquor shops, Rasheed smiled with his lips pressed together in respect and said in Hindi, "Brother, how are you doing today?" Usually, he came out of the stores with presents like packets of devil's food cakes or Twinkies, which we ate in the parking lot. I walked over to the store, waited by the aisle of chips and ramen, thinking over what I would say. The clerk's name here was Sameer, the silver tag his only jewelry. He was a pleasantly pudgy guy who spoke abruptly into his cell phone in what I suspected was either Hindi or Gujarati. My Tamil was decent because of my grandfather, while my Punjabi was more for decoration, words to adorn English sentences when I spoke to my father's relatives and friends. I learned a handful of Hindi phrases from Rasheed and the many Bollywood films his mother watched.

During class once a boy named Prakash turned to me and said, "Almost fifteen years ago, the Tamil Tigers killed Rajiv Gandhi, our great prime minister. You're part Tamil. Do you support terrorists?" He pressed his hand to his chest, pledging himself to the country, as if like him all of India loved to dance to Bhangra and eat chapati and dahl for lunch, and believed the Muslim actress Tabu was the sexiest, and Pakistan was a cesspool of thieves and wastrels.

English failed to be the official language of India by one vote, and my grandfather still cursed that decision, though he hated the English and blamed them for starting the civil war, uniting kingdoms, forming ragtag nations. Standing in the store, I felt speechless, words circling inside me just out of reach. When I finally settled on Hindi, I walked over to the man and said, "Aap Kaise ho."

He paused on his phone and asked, "How can I help you?"

"Aap Kaise ho," I repeated.

"Sorry, how can I help you?"

My hands were sweaty, and when I repeated the words again, I felt dumb and mute after he responded in what seemed like Hindi, his confusion looking more like concern at my lack of fluency in any language except this imagined one.

I shook my head and walked out of the store and didn't meet his eyes. I kept a slow pace so he wouldn't think I stole, but my mind was running, flipping through the sounds, wondering where I went wrong.

The lakeside was empty except for my brother and Gurmit treading water. I didn't know if they saw me, but I sat beside a trash bin watching them and feeling the sand slip between my fingers, all that wasted time. I fell asleep in that daze of regret as their bodies pushed through the water and the light disappeared behind the mountains.

If I heard them, I was far away, drifting from my body, but I was there and didn't stir when I heard my brother drowning. I hesitated and counted the breaths leaving him as I had once counted sheep in the darkness of our room. I stretched my hands out, spread my legs, and stood slowly while he fell below the surface. Thirty seconds, a minute, too long.

I first saw the hair in the water—a dark bloom of tendrils, belonging to a woman—move toward my brother as if to claim him, as if our ancestors could save us. But it was only Gurmit struggling through the water, clumsy as a manatee, showing me what I was about to lose.

I ran and scraped my knees to reach them and pull my brother to shore. We flipped him over and hammered his stomach until he vomited water. I was shaking, opening my mouth in half breaths like I was the one drowning. I waited for his eyes to open and for the world to begin. Gurmit stood to my side, his long hair dripping wet and clinging like algae to his hips, and I was on my knees, quiet, asking for mercy.

THE BUTCHER

THE BUTCHER SAT WITH BOTH his hands folded on the dinner table. It was the beginning of December, and he wore a tweed jacket and a white collared shirt. He had arrived without a hat or gloves, and Nalini had cried out from the doorway, "A butcher doesn't have enough fat in him for this cold." She grinned and held his frozen hands, leading him inside.

Marlon had known her for two years. She had floated in and out of the shop, ordering her weekly supply of meats and speaking now and then of her work at the hospital, her two boys, and the weather. Some days she came with her friend Rochelle, a concise woman with a slim waist and long acrylic fingernails that she often drummed across the metal counter while swaying her hips to a silent beat. "Marlon," she would say, "have any good men come in? All the men I get seem to be spoiled." She would look over at Nalini, and they would laugh. Nalini, in her blue nurse's uniform, would smile, collect her meat, and drop her few words like change into his tip jar.

Last week, when she invited him for a potluck, he was sitting on a stool, reading a letter from his wife, the blue paper thin and fragile in his hands. He was picturing his wife in their home in Gaborone, her wrists bright with bangles pressed against the paper. Though she was now married to another man and their daughter had been missing for four years, Marlon still called her his wife, a habit he could not break even when she started to address him only as Mr. Costa.

When he'd lifted his head, Nalini had looked at him expectantly. He told her he could use a pot of luck as she wrote down her address on the back of a receipt.

Now, dressed in his best suit, Marlon looked over the table. There was fish simmered in butter, a tray of rice, chicken with black bean sauce, and the lamb he had accidentally burned. Mr. Wu, who sat beside him, lowered his fork and announced that his son, Jiang, was returning home from his work in China at the telecommunication company. For five years, his now thirty-five-year-old son had been a disembodied head on a small rectangular screen echoing from the outskirts of Mr. Wu's childhood home of Beijing. The connection was often choppy, and Mr. Wu, impatient to hear from him, had once struck the screen of his phone, forever scarring his son's virtual face. For his last birthday, his son sent him a disc-shaped robot that glided across the carpet sucking dirt.

"I keep telling him I can die here anytime in my sleep like his mother, and he won't even know," Mr. Wu said, serving himself a mound of rice. "He'll be too busy strolling around the city of my beginnings to know my end."

Nalini's two sons, seated across the table, closed their eyes, playing dead, while their grandfather turned to Mr. Wu and shouted, "How wonderful."

Next to Marlon, a white man with big bones dressed in a brown suit politely nodded at the table. He had small eyes but a wide, generous mouth that Marlon imagined could gobble a whole fish in one gulp.

Nalini walked around the room, pouring wine into glasses. When she came to his spot, Marlon smiled, and for the first time all day his hands were still.

"When Jiang comes home," Mr. Wu continued, "everyone come next door to my house for a big feast."

The man in the brown suit nodded again and said, "That's so kind of you," and began to slice his fish. His name was Frank, and he was a surgeon. But he had such thick, heavy hands and such a squint that Marlon could not picture him holding a scalpel to any patient.

"So, Marlon," Frank mumbled, turning to the butcher. "You're from Africa, aren't you? I worked in Africa once after I finished my residency. It's a lovely place, poor place, but the landscape and the people are just vibrant."

"I'm Angolan, but I lived in Botswana," Marlon said and watched as Frank chewed on those foreign, unpalatable words.

"Well," Frank said, clearing his throat. "We were mostly in Uganda. Unfortunately, I didn't get to visit too many other places."

Marlon nodded. When he had come to America three years ago, relatives back home asked him if he lived by the Statue of

Liberty and the Golden Gate Bridge, and he would tell them he lived in central New Jersey and listen as their voices repeated the words, bewildered.

"Were you a butcher in Botswana?" Frank asked.

"I was an engineer."

"And now a butcher. Quite a jump, isn't it?"

Nalini stirred her glass. "Before that, he was a student. He's an expert on Samuel Johnson."

Marlon lowered his fork and wiped his mouth. She had caught him reading a book during a slow afternoon in the shop. She must have seen the bent cover, the folded pages, worn with his fingerprints, and known the unusual book was dear to him. Because she did not ask him what he was reading but why, and without meaning to, Marlon spoke of the English courses he had taken at the local college and a certain class that focused on major English texts.

It had been raining that day, and her coat was slick with water. She dried her hands against the lining, leaned forward, and lifted the book from his hands, the two flaps opening wide like the wings of a bird. He explained how he didn't finish his studies as she traced Johnson's oddly proportioned body with her finger.

He knew Nalini had completed college slowly, finishing her degree only after her marriage ended. Rochelle once said that Nalini did everything her own way. "She took night classes and worked during the day. She could read textbooks with her eyes closed."

Marlon's own education in America was not meant to last. His mother had used all their savings, mostly his own meager wages, to pay a year's worth of tuition to secure him a student visa. His wife had left him, and his daughter, forever seven years old, stayed framed on top of his mother's television set. The girl had her finger pointed at the camera, her face arched with a dash of attitude. "There is nothing here for you," his mother told him before she died, leaving him with no reason to return.

In those first months in New Brunswick, he drifted in and out of classes, taking English courses to improve his speech because his roommate, Kwame, had told him he had the stridency of a bullfrog. Kwame was a friend of a friend and lived near New Brunswick. His parents were both doctors and had arrived eighteen years earlier, becoming citizens, renouncing their passports from Ghana, and so Marlon did not understand why Kwame would provide a foreigner who had nothing to offer a place to stay. Standing in his apartment, he saw the unmade bed, the little furniture, the wooden cross on the wall, and knew Kwame lived alone. He was a short man, as small as a jockey, and some nights Marlon would awake to his dark image sipping water from a glass or sitting by the window, his eyes searching the streets, and Marlon's chest would tighten as he pictured a lost child.

Kwame found him the job at the butcher shop, and Marlon worked nights. He learned how to cut the meat, how to see through the skin and picture bones and organs so the knife moved in a knowing path. He had exchanged his work with engine fluid for animal fluid, but at least these poor creatures were dead and couldn't call out when he cut too deeply and punctured a lung or accidentally hacked off a piece of the heart. The manager was stingy and desperate for workers, and Marlon had no rent to pay and few needs. After a year, he was working full-time in the shop. At night and during the quiet moments in the day, he would pull out books and feel the heft of them in his hands. His favorite was his book on Johnson because the man was honorable but seemed so wretched. He was afflicted with sicknesses and tics that made him contort his face in a strange, frightening manner, and his jaw would spring open at the most inopportune times and release unworldly grunts. Still Marlon wished Johnson were alive today, though he would be two hundred ninety-five years old and even more wretched-looking. With him, Marlon thought, he could speak more freely.

Frank turned to Marlon and asked, "Didn't Johnson write the first dictionary?"

Marlon nodded. "And he gave refuge to prostitutes, and he had trouble with drinking." He paused and added, "He was a Christian." Even with that fact, Marlon knew his mother would not approve of Johnson for company.

The grandfather raised his glass and held it to the sky as if he expected God or the dead Johnson to pour him another drink. "How wonderful," he said. The younger boy, Karna, chirped after his grandfather: *How wonderful, wonderful, wonderful.*

When the boy quieted, Marlon still heard the faint echo of his words and remembered the warmth of the boy's hands around his neck. Earlier at the doorway, Karna had run up to him, his eyes wide and his fingers cupped over his mouth. Marlon bent to his knees, until he was the height of the boy, and Karna whispered into his ear, "Are you a giant?"

Marlon was a tall man, a little over six feet, a stature that earned him both respect and fear, currency a lonely man had little use for. But Kwame often praised his height. "Women will love you," he would say. "They will ask you how the air feels up there, and if you say you are a basketball player, they will fall at your feet." He even suggested marriage to an American woman so Marlon could get himself a green card.

The grandfather grabbed the dish of black lamb and started to eat the charcoal-colored meat, his jaw springing open after each bite.

"Lamb tastes—" the grandfather started.

"Wonderful," Arjun finished. "It tastes wonderful."

The grandfather reached over and slapped the top of his grandson's head, and the boy winced. But the old man kept his wrinkled hand there as a priest would for a blessing, and Arjun stayed quiet under the weight of it. He was the older of the two boys, only thirteen, but already he looked bruised from sleepless nights, his mouth twitching like some small, faint mammal.

"Let him be," Nalini said, and her father squinted at her, as though surprised to find her grown. He reached over for more wine, his hand shaking as he held the bottle.

Marlon had noticed a slight limp when the grandfather first greeted him. He shook Marlon's hand, and then his foot gave way under him, and he collapsed into Marlon's arms. He looked up at Marlon, not apologizing for his fall, as though he had always planned that long embrace. His companion, Mr. Wu, sat hunched in his chair, his back curved into the shape of a turtle's shell, his arms flabby and raw on his lap. He lived next door. When Marlon arrived, he noticed the two houses had fencing all around except between them, and Mr. Wu's garden spread into Nalini's yard, so in the spring one would only need to reach over for a fresh tomato or cucumber.

"Jiang tells me he's vegetarian," Mr. Wu said. "Now I don't know what to cook when he comes. He loved tofu stuffed with pork, beef and broccoli, fresh salmon and rice."

Frank looked over at Marlon. "Does the butcher have recommendations on vegetables?"

"I'm no good," Marlon said and pointed at his burnt lamb. He had been careless, waiting for a phone call from his wife instead of watching the stove.

"You know Rochelle is a vegetarian now," Nalini said, her eyes on Marlon. "She married her fitness trainer and moved to California, but I told her she would miss the New Jersey skyline too much and come running back."

Arjun laughed. "Fat chance."

It was the first time Marlon had heard of Rochelle in weeks.

She had stopped coming to the store, and Nalini never spoke of her. Now, without Rochelle, Marlon and Nalini had no one to fill in the empty spaces of their conversations. Marlon would look down at his hands on the counter, and Nalini would gaze at the assortment of meats. He secretly wished for Rochelle's arrival, for the easy chatter that came with her company. Like an aunt playing matchmaker, she teased Nalini and prodded Marlon into saying what they normally would not. Alone, on a busy day at the store, Rochelle had walked in wearing her hair wrapped in a scarf, and without warning him, she had leaned over the counter and kissed him on the cheek. "Take care of yourself, Marlon," she said, waving her engagement band at his shy face.

"It's supposed to snow today," Frank said and mopped his forehead with a napkin. "Have you ever seen snow, Marlon?"

Marlon put down his fork and looked out the window.

"Only a few inches."

Frank sighed. "Just wait, one of these days we'll get a blizzard."

The weatherman on the television had said it would snow. "This could be it, folks," the man said. "A white Christmas." The first time Marlon heard this, Kwame explained to him that white meant snow, not people, and then smirked as he pointed below at every white pedestrian on the street and cried out, "Christmas." It was two weeks until Christmas, but that was all people were talking about. Marlon saw customers come into the store with bags overstuffed with shiny paper, and when he went home, he listened to Kwame's one and only Christmas request: *A woman, that's all I want.* Marlon wondered how Christmas would be in Nalini's house, if they would have a tree and if the house would smell of cooking. When he was a child, his mother would take him to midnight mass. If he closed his eyes, she would squeeze his hand to make sure he was awake. When they returned home, she would hand him a present wrapped in an old comic-strip page from the newspaper and tell him stories of Baby Jesus until he fell asleep. Marlon's last three Christmases in New Jersey were spent with Kwame in front of the television. His friend would drink liquor and sing carols about St. Nick, the Fat White Man, who never visited their place.

Marlon now drank his wine quickly and felt a little liquid spill across his chin. He thought of his first time drinking with his then soon-to-be wife. She was only Alda then, and they drank from the same bottle, sharing that sweet-sour taste until they sucked the bottle clean. He had known her for seven months. She was a waitress in the café across from his office, and staring out the window, he noticed her eating her lunch alone on a roadside bench near a grove of motorbikes. With her napkin folded on her lap, she ate purposefully, not turning her head when a commotion broke out or someone kept their engine growling. He studied her and wondered how, after all his education, he had ended up in a cubicle inside a cement building, his head withered over his desk, reviewing reports of nautical vessels he would never travel on. From an early age, Marlon had been enamored with the sea, mostly from the stories his mother had told him of his grandfather, a Portuguese fisherman and brute who bathed each morning in the sea along with his kill.

Alda was made for land. She ate fruits like watermelons and oranges, and after a meal, she supported the seeds in one of her cheeks and walked up and down the dirt streets glancing from side to side. Only when he began to join her outside during her breaks did he see the way her lips formed a kiss, the seeds cushioned on her tongue as she blew. "Helping the babies grow," she said, and instead of thinking of gigantic pineapple plants and orange trees shooting out from the ground, he thought of a child, their child. The night before they were married they were reckless and smashed the wine bottle against a tree, too eager to consummate their union and slip into each other's arms. Marlon would remember that night throughout their marriage, the sourness of their breath like ripe fruit and their bodies dancing around glass shards.

AFTER DINNER, THEY moved to the living room. Nalini played the piano, and Arjun sat behind her on the carpet with a *National Geographic* magazine titled "Mountain Gorillas" on his lap. His hair covered his eyes, but he didn't bother with it and kept both his hands balled under his chin. On the couch, Frank leaned over to Marlon and asked if he knew any languages—Zulu, Swahili, Xhosa—because if he went to Africa again, he wanted to know how to say a few words. Mr. Wu told them to quiet down. He was listening to the music carefully and had closed his eyes. He held his hands out, dark with liver spots, each finger moving to the breadth of several notes, and though his hands shook, Marlon saw the aching intention with the stroke of each finger like tiny heartbeats pulsing.

Marlon looked around the house. The shelves were full of books, some in a different language. Tamil, he guessed, because Nalini had once written his name in Tamil, and he had thought, looking at those curved symbols, that they said more than just his name. There were photos hanging on the wall in floral frames, mainly of cats and boats, and he hoped to see the image of Nalini's ex-husband but all he could find were the pair of boys. His mother also did not have pictures of his father. He was God's child, she told him, although she had named him after Marlon Brando.

From the couch, Mr. Wu said, "Poor fingering. Play better," and Nalini nodded, bowing her head as she began to play more cautiously.

Marlon had never heard Nalini play before, but now that he had, he would hear the music when he sliced meat or took orders from customers or returned home on the bus. He would hear it even in perfect silence.

He closed his eyes, and there was only the sound of her playing, the soft shuffling of bodies around him. He could picture his daughter, Narissa, writing her lessons in her notebook, the sun dillydallying over her as her mother reviewed her arithmetic. *How are you going to grow up to be rich if you cannot even add?*

He remembered the way their daughter's things were divided between them. His wife kept most of her belongings, her dresses, shoes, drawings, photos, a seven-year-old accumulation, while he was left with everything his wife had deemed inappropriate for their daughter, a fly preserved in wax, bottles of nail polish, figurines of alien creatures. Marlon didn't argue with her. He gave her the house and stayed with his mother. He wanted to keep dividing himself until memory lost meaning, turned into an assortment of torn images. Two weeks later, his wife mailed him a children's book, Narissa's favorite, about two young girls who seem human until they discover their sealskin and return to the sea. On a half slice of paper, his wife wrote: *Maybe God thought I was too old to have a child, so this loss is either a gift or a curse. How long I wished to become a mother and I was granted it, or since I was once a mother, I will now always feel this unbearable absence.*

Marlon didn't know if the book was meant as a gift or a curse, if she had mentioned God as a friend or a foe. Certainly she had never cared for God before, and he wondered if their loss had shaken that skepticism or strengthened it, and if from now on his every thought would be cast in doubt that perhaps his wife was more faithful than he had supposed. Did he even know her? Or his daughter? He was the one who wanted to name the girl after a sea nymph. Did he fill her head with his dreams or were they her own?

• • •

THEY WERE IN the kitchen, refilling their glasses. Frank rolled up his sleeves and attempted to open a new bottle of wine. He rubbed his fingers together and gripped the neck.

"A stubborn little bastard, isn't it?" Frank said, his face reddening.

He had a cigarette behind his ear, and he paused to check if it was still there. He had spotted the cigarette in a vase of orchids and had kept it since, hiding it behind the curls of his red hair. "The grandfather," he whispered to Marlon, "has only got one lung left. But he can't quit." Frank eyed the bottle. "Can't survive with or without it."

"Do you smoke?"

Frank shook his head, and Marlon watched him, the gleam of his white arms, the deep scar that bloomed from under his left sleeve, narrowing into a sliver along his thumb.

Frank had reached over and swiftly pulled the bottle opener from the top of the fridge as if reaching behind his ear for the cigarette. There was an offhanded way about him that Marlon hadn't noticed when Frank sat stiff in his chair. He had left all his pleasantries at the dinner table, and now, holding the bottle, he cursed under his breath and laughed at his useless hands. He could have been young standing there, his face flushed, his hands fluttering over the cork, with all the expectation and awkwardness of first love.

"Success," Frank said with the groan of the cork. He smiled sweetly at the bottle, and for a moment, Marlon thought he might kiss it.

"How long have you been working at the hospital?"

"Almost four years."

"Do you like it?"

Frank blushed. "Yes, very much so."

They stood there, sipping from their glasses. Marlon could

hear the piano music from the other room and drank with the melody. If he strained his neck, he could see Nalini's arched back on the seat. Some days, at the store, when she walked to the door, he would imagine the feel of her spine against his palm and a hot shame would burn through his hand. Many days he kept his hand on the cutting block, the knife sharp and ready beside it. He had not thought of a woman in that way since his wife.

He had never been a handsome boy or expressive. Often his hesitation during conversations was mistaken as indifference, and at times he appeared cruel when he was very much infatuated. His mother said he'd grow up without knowing he had a tail unless he learned to bark. Sure enough, it took him three weeks, visiting the café every day, ordering porridge at the same time, before Alda's shift ended, for her to piece together his interest in her. She had gleaned from the few words he had shared with her before each meal that he was an engineer; his relatives, like hers, still called Luanda home; unlike her he had no siblings; he enjoyed the color of jade. Her uniform was a dull green.

"You're consistent," she said, and he didn't know if that was a compliment.

The time she was sick in the hospital, her uterus too ripe, swollen with blood, he sat beside her for long hours into the night, and she would awaken to see him there, his hands gripped between his knees and his eyes, unblinking, tired but determined. It was one of the reasons she married him, she said: his loyalty.

Now he felt like he was betraying the best part of himself because he couldn't stop thinking of Nalini. She would wear a dress, and he would see the firmness of her calves, and his heart would pound wildly like a cow or a pig being taken to the slaughter. He had never told Kwame about her because he didn't want him to imagine her with his other women, disrobing her in his dreams. Even if Marlon told Kwame, he knew what Kwame would say: *You are not a priest or a monk, so stop acting like one.* Though they recounted to each other every hour of their lives, Marlon did not fully trust Kwame because he was too honest, kept nothing to himself, laid out all his thoughts, from the perverse to the prosaic, for Marlon to view. Maybe he was lucky, though, to have a friend so plainspoken that in his excitement to tell Marlon some bit of news, saliva thickened in his mouth.

He turned to Frank, who was squinting into the darkness of the window. Frank finished his wine and licked his lips. "I miss the nights, the blackness of the savannah," he said and wiped his forehead with the back of his hand. "I was standing in the closed eye of the world, where everything was a dream, out of sight."

Frank brushed his scar, and Marlon tried not to stare.

"I had some shitty parents," Frank said and began to pour himself another drink, and Marlon noticed how Frank missed his glass, staining the countertop with wine. "I studied medicine, but still I can't help but think I inherited some of those genes for shittiness. And it's my duty not to multiply that shittiness in the world."

Since his daughter was dead, Marlon was certain he counted as a shitty parent, the end overshadowing the beginnings, when he would check his daughter's diapers for a healthy mustard color while his wife inspected her for defects and became more convinced over the years that their daughter was deaf. She would tell her to sit up straight and Narissa would squirm onto the floor like a worm. If she told her to keep her clothes clean, she returned gleefully stained in dirt and manure. His wife could not stomach the thought that her daughter might be unruly, stubborn even. "Did we have a son?" she said, staring at a dismembered doll on the floor. "What am I going to do with a girl like this?" During the first three years of her life, Narissa blabbered to the cows, the street dogs, a passing ant with a deference Marlon did not quite understand but nevertheless followed, tipping an imaginary hat to a sunbathing lizard or asking a perched owl about the weather. Narissa had the habit of pinching anyone, everyone, from the young to the elderly. On the bus she lifted the corner of a woman's blouse to grab a wedge of side fat, and the woman screamed until she noticed the little girl and looked toward Marlon in strict disapproval. When he sat Narissa down and told her about the intimacy of touch, she looked him straight in the eyes, pinched his cheeks, and stretched him into a smile, leaving only fleeting prints of her fingers like a good thief.

Marlon watched Frank finish three quarters of the wine and help himself to more. As he offered Marlon another glass, Frank peered into the other room, where the older boy hid himself under the tent of his magazine. From what seemed like the bottom of the bottle, Frank called out to him: "How are those mountain gorillas doing, buddy? We should go on a hike through the jungle sometime, buddy. Aren't we all a bunch of gorillas, buddy?"

All he received back was a pebble of a word. "Endangered."

"I'm forty-four," Frank said to Marlon, who was thirty-five, and they both looked at each other like they had very little time left on this planet.

The music had stopped. Mr. Wu was seated on the piano bench, readying his fingers as Nalini huddled over her father, her hands in his hands.

"Mr. Wu over there," Frank murmured, "plays the organ for his church."

The melody sounded, and Nalini pulled her father to his feet. He looked sheepish as she shuffled back and forth, swaying his arms. “Come on, come on,” Karna belted and bounced by the piano. Nalini and her father danced around the room. She led the way and he fumbled after her. His loose leg moved up and down, a painful spring. But he didn’t seem to mind it, and Nalini held his arms so tactfully that he didn’t notice her help.

She glanced over at Marlon, her hands intertwined with her father’s. Marlon beamed back and felt his spine straighten as if she were holding him up too. Earlier on the couch, Frank had told him that Nalini hardly ever touched the piano though she had brought it all the way from Kentucky, when it was only a hunk of wood with missing teeth and mangled chords, worth less than all the money she sank into it. “It’s probably because you’re here,” he said, and Marlon had looked down, his heart throbbing.

“Where’s Arjun?” Frank asked and moved toward the stairs.

Marlon stayed still. He didn’t want to leave the warmth of the room. He unbuttoned his jacket and leaned his head against the wall. He had rarely felt at home since he had arrived in America. Kwame did his best. He looked up recipes for Angolan dishes and hung a cloth wall to enclose the mattress on the floor. But now Marlon was not imagining the small apartment he would return to that night or picturing the house in Gaborone where his wife and another man would wake in the morning. They were too far to matter, and for once, the past and the future didn’t bother him. He was a butcher in America, and though there were countless other paths he could have taken, here he was, in the happy glow of strangers, and he wished to be nowhere else.

The room darkened and snow streamed past the window. Standing with his hand on the light switch, Karna cried, “How wonderful.” Marlon found himself echoing the boy’s words softly. He pictured the snow piling on top of the house, one layer after the other, burying them all in this blissful moment.

• • •

THE SNOW COATED the streets and the tops of parked cars. They stood by the window. A van turned into the road, its lights momentarily falling over them, their five faces lit against the glass.

"I'll play a nice holiday song," Mr. Wu said and returned to the piano bench. He patted the wrinkles on his shirt and straightened his sleeves. He did this without even looking, as though he had practiced these gestures countless times before. "Jiang's favorite," he added. He removed his watch and placed it on the ledge of the piano and began to play. Marlon listened but didn't look at Mr. Wu's fingers, which must have pained him. His own hands nowadays felt sore. After work, he would massage them in a bath of warm water until they were wrinkled and plump but relieved. He wondered what Mr. Wu did to calm himself, and he tried to imagine Mr. Wu's life beyond this moment.

Outside the snow gathered speed. Mr. Wu paused from his playing to speak of the grace of winter. The grandfather shook his head. "The snow is not God's miracle," he said. "If it were a miracle, it would melt from the driveway and the sidewalk without me having to shovel."

It was getting late. The buses ran until midnight, but with the snow, it was likely they would stop earlier. Then Marlon would have no choice but to walk or stay over. He wanted to stay over. He wanted to fall asleep in the house and wake to breakfast and the sound of the children. Marlon opened the front door, and a sharp wind cut its way into the house. He couldn't tell how much snow had fallen, but he felt the cold and saw how the white hid everything, and he thought he was somewhere else. From the living room, Nalini shouted, "Close the door." He did and heard her voice straighten out. She had never raised her voice to him before. It made him feel oddly anxious and excited, and he kept by the door and dared not return and see her. Whenever he upset his wife, she would not speak to him, simply occupy her hands, but in one glance, he could sense the color of all her other feelings; even anger needed affection and longing to surface. Waiting by the doorway, he could feel the heat in his face. The light of the living room suddenly seemed too bright and revealing, so instead he climbed the stairs, stood in the dark hallway.

Through the crack of an open door, he saw Arjun lying on his bed, his head rested on the pages of a book and his eyes fixed on the ceiling. His arms were wrapped around his waist. Marlon thought the boy looked solemn lying there in his dress shirt and trousers that did not seem to suit him, that had all the appearance of someone else's doing. He remembered the undertaker of his boyhood, who readied corpses with his piggish fingers, applying blush to bloodless cheeks. He remembered the coffins, the deep smell of wood mixed with perfume, the bodies of loved ones strangely still. He remembered how his daughter had never had her face painted by an undertaker or had her mother dress her in her birthday frock. And that there was no grave, no coffin that held her body.

Arjun turned to his side and stuck his fingers under the mattress and pulled out a photograph. He sat up and held it at eye level like a hand mirror. He didn't look away.

Marlon moved deeper into the hallway. Near the end was a large window where he could see the moon and the falling snow. The streets were now caked with it, and he could no longer find the black of the asphalt. It comforted him, the way the snow drifted into the night. He wanted to run outside and feel the cold against his skin and cool his thoughts of love. He could still feel the touch of her hands on his wrist and hear her voice telling him to hold still. He had once cut his hand after he had spent an hour in the freezer and served a woman extra-bloody veal slices. He hadn't noticed, his skin hard and cracked like a frozen glove. Nalini had cleaned the wound with the first aid kit he had found in the back of the store. She held his hand carefully and showed him how to wrap the bandage. It was the first time they had talked.

After that meeting, he started thinking of marriage again. His mother had never approved of his marriage to Alda. The girl was older and had been married before, but that didn't really matter. It was the fact that she was a nonbeliever his mother couldn't handle. "If she doesn't believe in God, then what is life good for," she would say. "She has beliefs," he would mutter. Though, at the time, he could name only one unutterable belief. *Me*, he wanted to tell his mother. *She believes in me.*

He didn't know what his mother would have thought of Nalini. He didn't know if she was a religious woman, but there were days at the store when she would stand by the counter, her eyes closed as he readied her meats, and he knew that she was praying. Because wasn't prayer a moment of relief, in which that lonely burden of hopes was shared? Because when she looked at him, her eyes clear, he knew he had been praying too.

He looked around the dark bedroom. The moonlight spilled through the window, and he could see the vanity table with perfume bottles and brushes. By the mirror, there was a peg holding a tangle of necklaces. He grazed his hand against them and listened to the chime of the metal. The brass handle of a door glistened beside him. He twisted until inch by inch he was bathed in a foamy light.

Frank was seated on a closed toilet in a T-shirt and boxers. His shoulders slouched over his knees as he smoked a cigarette. Above him the window was open and when he stood, he blew his breath outside, but the smell had seeped into the walls, a tea-stained color. The grandfather would be blamed, Marlon supposed, and the old man with one lung probably wouldn't care, already committed to dying on his own terms. When Frank turned, Marlon could see the man's round, lumpy knees like scoops of vanilla ice cream melting. He looked then like a man who didn't expect much of his life, jaw trembling, reeking with secrets. Marlon apologized, shut the door without making a sound.

MARLON WAS FINISHING his tea when Frank opened the front door and was greeted with a rush of snow. Frank wore a fox-tailed fur hat and a forest green coat that reached his knees. It was lined with golden buttons down the center in the style of a general's uniform. He looked over at the two boys and with the command of his wrist, he pointed at the coatrack and signaled them to hurry. Karna trooped outside without a jacket, only to return shortly at his mother's insistence and grab his blue puffy coat from the closet. Marlon sat on the couch, holding his cup, the heat still lingering in the porcelain while Arjun, beside him, silently flipped through a magazine. Frank stared at the boy, but he never looked up and continued to give each page a purposeful slap to the next.

Frank strolled over to Arjun's side and, without a word, lifted him into the air. The boy looked momentarily terrified, his whole weight balanced in another man's hands. He didn't protest, just kept still—a sign of trust or defeat? Marlon wondered—as the chill night air settled on them. Frank lowered the boy to the ground and walked toward the doorway, looking back once before he left.

Arjun pieced himself together. He sat down and rubbed his shoulders where Frank had held him and returned to his magazine. He turned a page, and his face tensed, considering some text. After a long pause, he dropped the magazine, reached for his coat, and walked outside.

There were eight houses on the street, each with the same

rectangular porch and low roof. No one outside except for them, the warm light of the other houses casting shadows on the snow.

Marlon moved to the porch, but Mr. Wu and the grandfather stayed inside because they'd both had enough snow to last a lifetime. Mr. Wu said this with great pleasure while the grandfather only grunted. The others were constructing a snowman. They packed the powdered snow into fleshy clumps and collected fallen twigs, hidden under a thicket of pine needles. The snow streamed around them, hiding fractions of their faces, the small details Marlon wanted to see. When Nalini said she hadn't made a snowman in so long, he couldn't tell if Frank was smiling, but he knew he was looking at her.

They finished the body of the snowman and all they had left was the head. Frank stood next to the snowman and compared his own waist with the cold creature's. "He's fitter than I am," he said and continued to pat snow down on its cool belly. He didn't wear gloves and kept warming his skin with his breath. He touched Nalini's cheeks with his hands, and she screamed, running from him.

Marlon imagined Alda sitting by his side, here on the front porch of America, the heat of her neck resting against him. After her first marriage, to a young man who labored at a petrol station, she wouldn't have wanted to be tied down to a butcher. *Dirty work*, she'd say, though they both knew money never came clean.

He bought her a pair of golden track shoes on their wedding day. He wore his black Adidas. They were running off together, eloping, both amused at the sight of each other. She, a godless divorcée with a womb made of dried clay, and he, raised by a single mother and too young to even know what a marriage looked like.

The church was plain except for its elaborate wooden beams and trusses. The roof full of holes and the aisle wet when they walked down it, but the room shimmered with coin-sized rays of light. Besides the gardener and an elderly woman acting as witnesses, the birds were their only guests and flanked both sides of the room and cawed as he tripped on her dress, and they both tumbled to the priest.

Marlon had not attended church since that day or taken Communion. Perhaps, he thought, he could join Mr. Wu's church. He would listen to Mr. Wu play the organ and return home with him, and together they would visit Nalini, her father, and the boys.

Frank came over and sat on the porch steps. He blew into his pale hands and tucked them into his pockets. He kept turning to Marlon, meaning to say something, but he didn't.

Marlon watched Frank's shoulder quiver and remembered the sight of his knees.

"Do you come here often?" Marlon asked.

"Well, yes," he said. "I have known Nalini for three years."

Marlon had known Nalini for only two years, and this was his first time at her house.

"You're not married," Marlon said, and he did not mean for his words to come out as an accusation, but they did.

Frank looked at him closely, and there was something tender in his face. "No, I never was. And I didn't know if I wanted to be."

"Do you know now?"

Frank blinked and looked down at his scar. "Nalini told me you were married."

Marlon's cheeks burned from the mention of his own marriage. "I was married for nine years," Marlon said, and Frank nodded gently.

He never thought of his marriage with a beginning and an end, the short span of a child's life. They could not return to being simply husband and wife. They were both widowed; his wife would look at Marlon and remember he was once a father, and he would look at her crying into her tea and know she would never be a mother again.

His daughter could hold her breath for almost a minute, and this thought had kept him breathing as he swam through the choppy water searching for her. That day on their trip to the shore, watching her carve the sand into half-melon breasts she did not yet possess, he had noticed her giggling privately to herself in a satisfied and unguarded way, her whole body trembling with unknowable delight. When she climbed onto his back, her arms tight around his neck, he felt her mouth warm against his cheek as he pushed into the water. Then in one step, one breath, a wave cleaved them into two, and when he broke the surface of the water and couldn't see her, he felt a sharpened sense of his body, the persistent piercing of his chest, the filtering of his blood into good and bad. As he dove again and again into the water grasping for time, the past and the future drifted into the horizon.

His wife had no god, only a haggard and hollow-eyed husband who, refusing mirrors, had to rely on the woman to trim his hair and beard while he spoke of time travel, recalled the flying machines he had dreamt of as a young boy. His wife lamented, called Marlon's mother. "I have lost a child, and now your son has turned into a child."

He knew his neglect, his shabbiness, had given his wife more reason to find nourishment elsewhere. She needed the solid assurance of the world, a stone she could hold in her hand.

Years before, she had come home to tell him a miracle had happened and pressed his hand against her belly that had been barren for so long. In the afternoon light, she carried the radiance of the Virgin Mary, and pouring water from a drinking mug, he baptized her in the tub, a miniature deluge pooling around his ankles, and in the morning the cracks between the boards contained spots of mold.

"Do you think you'll marry again?" Frank asked after Marlon told him he wrote letters to his wife every week, though she rarely answered them.

"I don't know. But Johnson said marrying again is the triumph of hope over experience."

"And do you believe that?"

"Yes, I hope I do."

"God bless you."

Marlon looked at Frank, suddenly annoyed. He wished Frank would leave quickly, but Frank took his time and warmed his hands by his mouth before he dug them back into his pockets. The snowman was still headless. Karna placed two short branches into the sides of the belly for arms. Marlon shivered, and Frank looked at his bald head and handed him his fur hat. But Marlon wouldn't take it. What did it matter that Frank had a bush of red hair and he had nothing?

"Doctor's orders," Frank said and tossed his hat on Marlon's lap as he returned to the snowman and all those waiting for him. Marlon dropped the hat and followed Frank, eclipsing each of Frank's footprints with his own.

Now no one bothered with finishing the snowman. Nalini propped her head on the snow-body, becoming part of it. The boys threw handfuls of snow at each other. Karna caught the remains of a snow grenade in his mouth and burst open with laughter. Marlon chased after the boys until they tumbled, and together they found frosted pinecones and launched them into the air.

When Marlon turned, a snowball hit his chest. Nalini jumped from behind the snowman, and he watched as her smile faded as if she had been saving it for someone else. "I'm sorry. I didn't mean to—"

Marlon waved off the apology and brushed his chest. When he leaned down to pack clumps inside his fist, he felt his chest tighten and thought it was best to rest and walked back to the porch. All the elation that had held him up a moment ago left him, and he sat with a wilted spine, his hands bent over his knees. It was pity. All pity he had mistaken for love.

He saw it then: Nalini's face above the counter, inviting him for dinner. He remembered how he had told her his Christmas plans, and how she must have inwardly cried for his poor self, retelling all the sad details of that future evening to Frank. He imagined them talking about him, locked in each other's arms.

It was not her fault. He should have known. They had exchanged occupations before names. "I'm a nurse," she said to him, the butcher, as she wrapped his hand.

He wondered now if he looked like the man in the bathroom. If his jaw trembled and his arms shook, and if he looked both sad and frightened, crouched low to his knees as though gazing into an empty coffin. He let the snow wet his face in streaks, knowing this would be his last time at the house. Pity only stretched so far, to the confines of a butcher shop and an occasional invitation.

The snow continued, unabated. Under the streetlamp, Frank walked toward Nalini, his red hair sopping wet like a morning rose. From inside, Mr. Wu started to play the piano, and Marlon heard the music and could anticipate every beat that was to follow: Frank would marry Nalini; Mr. Wu would be reunited with his son; the grandfather would smoke and smoke. And Kwame would be at home, ready with a story. He stood up, took one last look at everybody before he turned toward the quiet of the street. He had spent a lifetime loving strangers.

LIFETIMES IN FLIGHT

I DO NOT PRAY ANY LONGER, but some evenings, when I return home from my work at the library, the sight of the sun descending will make me fall to my knees in ritual and think of my father on his prayer mat, his legs squared underneath him, his head pressed firmly to the ground, and I rise with him remembering the fragility of his face, composed from no more than bird bones. The pink shells of his lips coil tight and then part for my name.

In the summer of 1951, my fourteen-year-old father, Selvakumar Choudary, hid away in a cargo ship and traveled from Ceylon to South India, returning to the homeland of his great-grandfather. Though my father never knew the man, it was his memory he held on to when he ran away from the tea plantation and took possession of his life.

The story went that his great-grandfather was born near the Meenakshi kovil in Madurai, and seventeen years later as he rolled tobacco leaves and drank on the roadside he saw in the waning moonlight the goddess pass through the archway of the temple. He was not religious, though he regularly met with astrologers to argue about their predictions of his future. "You will never leave Madurai," one jothidar had pronounced faithfully, a hand pressed against the alignment of celestial bodies, and my great-great-grandfather slapped the jothidar with such ferocity the man simply sat stunned and quiet in the daze of his words.

He was striking down the future he did not care for and perhaps the sight of the goddess, the manifestation of true beauty, awoke in him a longing, carried since birth, for the deep embrace of the unknown. Later when he left as a laborer for Ceylon, he married a woman he met at the plantation named after the goddess, a cripple who dragged her right leg.

Maybe it was the image of the divine claiming his great-grandfather or how his own origins were revealed to be in that ancient Indian city, so even when parliamentary acts were passed that disenfranchised my father of the vote he was not yet old enough to cast, revoked his citizenship, my father thought of himself belonging elsewhere, to where the heavens met earth.

My father never set foot in Madurai. All his great plans for his arrival in India soon came apart once he reached the shores of Rameshwaram, a town of churches and fishermen. In the distance he'd see the tip of his island and feel an emptiness as dark and deep as the sea, knowing he had left before understanding that ancestral word: *home*.

Back at the tea plantation my father picked leaves, labor he might have called painstaking if he had not walked across the flat streets of Rameshwaram, his bare feet hardened by dust, as he carried granite for construction. He lived in a single room with three other boys. The oldest, Anand, was soft-spoken with an evenhanded melancholy. "When you're poor," he'd say, "you're never going to belong anywhere." He had a blue glass eye, which terrified and astonished my father, reminding him of Sir William from the tea plantation, so that at night my father slept full of longing for his old, familiar suffering on the hillside.

The two other boys, Yogesh and Bhushan, were twins, both first cousins and brothers. Their mother had given Yogesh away to her barren sister, and though raised apart the boys resembled each other in stance and manners. They crossed their arms while they sat and sneezed loudly with their heads thrown back from too much sunlight. Both possessed an imaginative cruelty and on a single afternoon they sat around and crushed chicken skulls with their palms and fashioned the bones into dice. Only with the structure of their jaws did they part ways. Yogesh's underbite left him eating soft things, ripe bananas and boiled rice.

Together they worked on the building of a house for a wealthy politician, who had dubbed himself Lenin in honor of the Russian communists, who were popular at the time in Tamil Nadu. Lenin sold pieces of inherited land to anyone, regardless of caste or religion, granted four acres of green forest to missionaries to open a school and a quarter acre for a mosque and poultry farming. He took an interest in the poor, he said, and scribbled out loans with enough interest to leave men naked and penniless.

The first time my father saw Lenin he was dressed in a striped velour suit. He was balding but not nearly as unattractive as my father expected. Because of his relentlessness—determined to wear a fashionable suit in the tropics, craft everything, all his furniture included, from pure sandalwood, no matter the cost to him or to the surrounding forests—my father understood that he should never cross the man.

Only around his wife did Lenin seem puerile, vulnerable. When the house was near completion, she arrived at the construction site in an emerald green silk sari, her hair plaited and rolled into a bun, a honey orchid bursting from the crown of her head. In the harsh, dry summer months she carried an umbrella and looked exotic, part of the wild of some distant place. With each visit to the house, she voiced a new complaint, and the men worked hours overnight changing the wooden flooring to granite, and the next day upon her request, they would rip open the ground to shuffle the wood back into place. The woman was beyond pleasing and no one knew if her insatiable displeasure was for the house or her husband. Without saying a word, Lenin would fall to his knees, call her his little peacock. His trouser bled brown as she relished the sight of the wealthiest man in the district groveling at her feet. She once slapped him with her foot and simply walked away, Lenin fumbling after her from his knees.

During these occasions Bhushan was watchful. He would stop working as she passed. The solid rock of dirt he held in his hands would be no different from his heart, carelessly given, almost tossed away. Bhushan was known for his temper, so no one expected the patience of a letter, a love letter more precisely, slipped in the crack of an unfinished window. Fifteen letters were discovered by Lenin. In response he ordered Bhushan to be whipped fifteen times with his own belt. "You must not let your eyes wander from your duties," he instructed Bhushan, but his eyes glinted with an unbridled pleasure, for he enjoyed other men coveting what he had. It added value to his possessions. In the raw center of his beating, Bhushan kept turning toward the house, thinking if she could see him, he would be saved.

That night Anand smeared turmeric paste on the three darkest welts strung along Bhushan's back. Yogesh moaned, holding his head, as though he had been beaten too. Bhushan, usually shameless with his anger, seemed subdued, sprawled on the floor as if some stray feeling inside him was sheltered.

My father asked Bhushan if he loved the woman, and Bhushan cracked his fingers. "That slut," he said, but he was grinning.

In the morning, it was decided that they would rob Lenin. The following month they cut masks from cloth purses and each carried a machete the size of an arm.

"Do not kill anyone," Anand said. "Unless." He paused and my father heard his own death in that silence.

The house was built in the seclusion of a few trees and acres of parched land. Neighbors needed to walk seven minutes to reach his two-story house. Lenin slept on the bottom floor while his wife, his mother, and his sick sister resided upstairs near a canopy of tender coconuts. Outside a gateman kept watch. He was an old man who after dinner carried his teeth in his palm. He had cataracts that tinted the world into the airy color of heaven. Around his neck was a medallion with a picture of Jesus Christ. When he saw four shapes move past the gate, machetes blinking brightly against the lanterns, he believed he saw holy spirits coming for him and he closed his eyes in anticipation.

They crept through the back and up the stairs into a room where the women sat together reading a newspaper by a lamp.

Yogesh closed the door, brought his machete to his lips, and told them to be quiet. Yogesh and Bhushan spoke loudly in Tamil and Hindi, mixing the languages with a made-up one.

"Where's the jewelry?" Anand asked. When they didn't answer, he dragged his machete across a bedsheet and sliced it into two.

The grandmother motioned to the wardrobe. Her wrinkles were like loose chains. "The key opens the last drawer to the cabinet where we have everything," she said.

My father unlocked the drawer and pulled out gold earrings, ruby-studded bracelets, a diamond belt, and dropped them in a gunnysack.

"Now your thalis," Anand said, and Yogesh hooked the machete in the air near their throats until all their wedding necklaces were removed. The single fat gold nugget on each hung like a shrunken head. Lenin's younger sister, still unmarried at the age of thirty-nine, sat staring at the necklaces with a glimmer of envy.

Bhushan stood in the corner of the room beside the wooden table, which held a ceramic vase and lantern, streaks of blue light on the wall. He held his machete limp in his hand, and when the others left, he removed his cloth mask. Perhaps he was convinced if the wife saw him, she would understand how he felt. But I think it was arrogance that made him bring the lamp close to his face and leave a print of his features on their memory.

Downstairs they found two lakhs hidden beneath a statue of Lord Ganesh, and they each prayed before taking the money. Before they left, the grandmother, obscured beside her son's rotund, whimpering presence, requested her thali be returned. She asked casually with the expectation of a mother talking to her son.

Anand handed the two necklaces back. "Forgive me," he said. "We did wrong."

On their way back home, Yogesh shoved Anand in the chest. "We could have made good money with that gold."

When my father emptied the sack onto the floor, he thought of his dreams where all the leaves he picked turned into treasure. The metals clinked against one another, and they danced through the night, embraced by the warm ground like men of this world.

After the robbery they returned to work normally, afraid to cause any alarm. In a week's time, the police arrived and arrested them. "You cannot fight fate," Yogesh said to Anand while they sat in the station. "Some people are lucky and some are not."

Lenin's wife was asked to identify one of the assailants, and without hesitation she pointed at Bhushan, and he grinned, for he must have thought she had chosen him for a better fate.

They would never know completely how they were discovered but later learned pieces: Bhushan's betrayal, a forgotten sapphire ring their neighbor had discovered. But they must have known that they had lost earlier, from the beginning.

Instead of sending them to court, the sergeant said he would mete out the punishment. He and two other officers beat them to varying degrees according to their temperament. Bhushan received the harshest treatment. He was slammed against a table and a chrome bar gnashed his face. At the end he looked no different from Yogesh. My father was spared with only a broken arm.

WHEN MY FATHER was sixteen, he was adopted by his employer, Mr. Gopal, a retired English professor at Saint Mary's. My father was first hired to complete small tasks outside the house. He retrieved the paper, milked the cow, and tended the garden with an alacrity belonging to obligation, but perhaps Mr. Gopal saw in those duties acts of love. Soon my father was allowed deeper inside the house, and he explored the chambers of the dining room and the kitchen before he went upstairs to the bedrooms and then farther up to the roof, where he could stand and see the ocean.

My father must have found his way into the old man's affection, opening each door, discovering each room with an unknown excitement from his years of living in one room.

Mr. Gopal had never been married, though he had loved two women in his lifetime. He was the son of a merchant but had squandered much of the wealth with mismanagement of the business and his desire to partake in the lewd discussions of philosophers and artists. A staunch communist in his youth, he eventually became convinced of the inertia in the movement. He studied abroad in Cambridge all the classic poets, Keats, Blake, Eliot, and his father railed against him. "How will we ever defeat the British if you're reciting after their hearts and souls?"

At the age of seventy-three, he tired of people and wrote daily letters to the dead. He burned messages with flowers in the early mornings as offerings, the ash carrying the scent of hibiscus and carbon. It was the closest he came to religious belief.

When he decided my father would be his son, it was done quietly without fuss, the shake of his hand across some opal-tinted papers.

Mr. Gopal spent his mornings reading and in the afternoons he walked to the tea stall and slowly sipped two cups, listened to the gossip of men, and shouted at their foolishness. My father accompanied him, and Mr. Gopal would turn to him and smile with his blackening gums. "No one bothers you when you're old." Returning from a trip to the market with my father,

Mr. Gopal once paused outside a temple where a pujari bent to pour milk over a Shiva lingam. "Why do we feed the gods milk and ghee?" he asked. "Do they hunger like we do? Do they die?"

My father always thought of his life in Mr. Gopal's house as precarious. He thought the old man would wake and forget his presence, denounce him as an intruder. Perhaps that is why on occasion my father stole from Mr. Gopal. First it was the pair of bronze elephants he found on a shelf and then a finely carved wooden Shiva statue. When he was more daring, he pilfered a pair of gold mango-shaped earrings from a locked cabinet. He amassed a collection of stolen goods, which he kept under a loose floorboard. He had not realized, as Mr. Gopal's son, that all this already belonged to him.

In the springtime Mr. Gopal asked him to keep his eyes out for the missing earrings, for they belonged to someone special. Mr. Gopal had not accused him, but he must have known. When my father ran off with a bottle of toddy, a store clerk wrung him by the neck, and Mr. Gopal defended him, shielded the boy with his voice. Mr. Gopal still wore his reading glasses and the sun illuminated the outline of his eyes.

He taught my father to read in English, though he never sent him away for schooling, which strikes me now as both generous and selfish. The way one might protect a seed but never plant it.

Only later, nearing his end, did Mr. Gopal reveal his intention for my father's marriage. The girl was the daughter of his old schoolmate from Cambridge. They had both worked as clerks in West Bengal and fallen in love with the same woman, the cook's daughter. She had chosen his schoolmate, and Mr. Gopal in turn broke all relations and his resentment sustained him through his old age even after learning of their premature deaths.

Perhaps he intended the marriage between the poor orphaned

daughter and my father to rectify the past. The girl lived with an aunt's family in Madras, and she must have married my father without better prospects.

Mr. Gopal bequeathed his house and the remains of his wealth to my father, including his cow, but in his last moments of life, when candlelight shrouded his face, he beseeched my father to take my mother's surname, Choudary, a Bengali name, for a Tamil one, Govindasami. He then closed his eyes and surrendered with each exhale. His skin hung loose like rings of dried wax, his lips still as a leaf, and in the morning he died in the explicable way men do.

In the single marriage photo I possess, my mother is a full head taller than my father. She is looking to her side, and her mouth is parted in an expression of indifference or maybe disappointment. I never asked my mother what she saw at that moment.

She was sixteen, a year younger than my father, when she married. As a child, my mother slept on goose feather pillows, played backgammon, and accompanied her father to see picture shows, and in her precise and ordered life, she must not have seen herself tied to my short-statured father, a tea-picker, a thief, the great-grandson of a cripple.

She was a beauty for the rareness of her features, milky skin, green eyes, all ordinary to her each time she sat by the mirror, and only after an outing filled with whistles and mustache-raising stares did she sense the value of her body. She once spent a week of my father's wages on silk saris. With all her selfishness I do not think she despised my father but the cruelness of fate.

The child she gave birth to was not a consummation of their marriage but the arrival of a second life. She was being born again. Alone with the baby, she told stories, remembered how to laugh as she held her finger out for the child to suck. My father caught them together in their secluded intimacy, where my mother spoke in Bengali, sounding the words like a secret lullaby.

In 1955 they abandoned Mr. Gopal's house and moved to Calcutta. Their fortune resided with the land but my parents had not been prudent. If they had sold it, maybe our lives would have been different. In their absence, the property was annexed by the town council for the construction of a six-floor hotel with a luxury pool. My mother wanted to return to West Bengal so urgently that she was willing to trade her life for a poorer, more uncertain one.

She would regret her decision to leave for Calcutta and come to regard the city with an instinctive distrust, but for a year and a half she was content simply to sit by the street with her daughter on her lap and listen to gossip as she settled into the rhythm of those warm days. For a brief time my mother and father must have sensed within each other the respite they had both longed for all those years. I doubt my presence ever brought them close to that rare glimpse of satisfaction, when they reached for each other with the ease of a happy family.

ON OCTOBER 23, the night of the Kali Puja, three men released a pig into a mosque during evening prayer and in retaliation men armored themselves with rage and sharp steel. Some carried their mothers' kitchen knives while others measured out the deadly angle of a cricket bat. My father ran down Park Street and toward the center of the city holding the limp body of his one-and-a-half-year-old child.

There were no faces out at night, only shadows of bodies: uncircumcised and circumcised, red dot and no red dot, Hindu and Muslim, human and human.

That night, after my father wrapped his daughter in his

wife's silk sari, he roamed the city, drunk on spilled baby's blood. He held his hands out to the sky and black crows perched on the edges of buildings looked down at him and cawed. Gripped in that lonesome embrace, my father waited for signs, his own moment of revelation promised by his great-grandfather's vision of the goddess in Madurai. What my father saw was a bow-legged man wearing a skullcap stumble out of a hovel of sheet metal and planks into an empty alleyway leading to the road. He did not follow the man but paused by the house composed of discarded waste salvaged and arranged in an unsightly balancing act. Standing at the entrance, he slipped his hand behind the cloth curtain, as alluring as a lady's skirt, and saw the shape of a woman through the burn of the kerosene lamp. She slept curled around a bundle of blankets, hiding her child but not the wet, hungry murmurs of the night air.

My father knew the sounds of his child and lifted the baby, a girl no older than a year. She opened her mouth and showed the soft grasp of her tongue, pure pink pleasure, and grabbed his thumb and fed on his skin. As he rocked the girl, he thought of the sparrow with one wing he had cared for as a young boy. He touched her chin and the undersides of her brow, tracing a smooth curve of love until he felt only the absence.

In that touch his hands were no longer his as he disappeared, becoming a Hindu priest breaking open a coconut sacrifice. He smashed the child against the ground in the name of a dead baby, in the name of God.

The facts are like bones that tell me nothing but the end. I wonder when my father chose me if he saw any likeness to his daughter or to the other child. In his grief he must have picked more simply, without any recollection. Because the Sisters had no record of my parents and I was the youngest in the orphanage, only eight months, I was the easy choice, the closest to rebirth. That day I was born from two dead babies. Named after the goddess Saraswati and raised as a Muslim.

I am a librarian in Essex, and I think my father would have found Essex to his liking, the distant wail of seagulls from the shore and the calm nights. He preferred to pray in the early mornings, when the streets were quieter, but nowhere in Calcutta is silence absolute. Even then, dogs howled in maddening bursts and men stood around, lazily slapping the air with chatter as women bargained for fruits and meat, and my father would rush outside with a hand covering his eyes as if he wished to shun the world.

My mother slept through his prayers and the commotions of daily life. When she awoke, she was restless and walked around our small three-room home, unsure of her bearings, stared at the peeling walls with memories of expansive corridors and archways of her childhood. I dressed in my blue uniform and left for school and in the afternoon returned before she noticed my absence. She mostly remained in the house. My father said she was ill, but I don't recall her with a fever or nausea; rather I remember her fair skin, smooth and golden like the inside of a jackfruit. I would brush my arm against hers, and she would wince. Later when I understood her daughter's death, I wondered if my presence frightened her, the way I called her Ma, running my teeth against it until she answered.

My father would return from his work at the printers and embrace me smelling of ink. Holding me, he'd say I was Allah's miracle, and I would tug at his beard and his mouth would curve into a frown at my command. On my right hand, I have six fingers. My father said Allah had been too generous with me. But when I looked around our home, fistfuls of light pouring from the roof, the posters of my mother's favorite actor, Uttam Kumar, covering the latest damage to the walls, I never felt certain. My father called our home the Great Taj. Everything appeared larger, more complete in my father's eyes.

Outside I hid my right hand under my school clothes. I trained myself to write with my left hand though it was discouraged and having six fingers was blessed. My mother kept in her cabinet a red-handled Swiss Army knife along with all her other belongings. The cabinet with its dark splintered wood was the only substantial furniture in the rooms, and many times I caught myself on the edge, a cheek or a shoulder emblazoned with soreness, deeper than a kiss.

Pain did not trouble me then like embarrassment did. There were days I thought I would die from it and held my belly as though nursing a bullet wound. Under the shade of a fig tree behind our school, I asked my classmate Shamala to cut off the accursed finger with my mother's pocketknife. I did not trust my left hand for such a delicate task. Shamala was a quiet student and wrote in such neat and careful handwriting that I was certain her fingers would trace a clean cut, wordlessly. But she surprised me and screamed when I showed her the blade, ran off into the street, her braid unraveling with her voice.

I did not have close friends and when my mother scolded me for taking the knife, I had nowhere to retreat, and waited instead for my father, knowing I'd hear the sound of the chains on his bicycle before seeing him. He looked no older than a child, my thirty-two-year-old father. The bicycle loomed beside him like a nickel-colored horse, and I would see my father's true size. A stature my mother associated with his early childhood work as a tea-laborer.

On hearing my misdeed, he did not punish me but lowered his head in prayer. He looked at me, his features puckered in pain as if I had slid my mother's knife across the gash between his lips.

We sat in the back of the house with a lantern, and my father revealed a new book he had brought home from work. Before opening the cover, he let me touch the spine and watched me as he smoked a beedi. Flipping through the pages, I held my nostrils close to the wave of paper and smelled the pigment. I imagined my father working with the printers, changing gears, feeding paper into the machines, and I hoped a splotch of black might mark me.

We read books in English and Bengali. My English was poor then, as I knew only a handful of phrases, but my father spoke fluently, or rather unashamedly. I fear if I heard his words now, I might find them unacceptable. Though his mother tongue was Tamil, I rarely heard him speak the language. He had only a few memories of his own grandparents or cousins. Neither my father nor my mother safeguarded their histories. They carried memories carelessly. "How many first cousins do you have?" "Five, maybe four," my father would answer.

When they spoke in Tamil, the words flew around me but felt mysteriously intimate, and I imagined them professing love they rarely showed.

On the day of the incident with the finger, my father showed me an encyclopedia of birds. Ospreys, whistling ducks, gray-headed fish eagles. Each chapter opened with a finely detailed portrait of a bird with lines pointing to different body parts. Initially, my father brought home books by Western philosophers like Descartes; later ecology books about the Arctic and the Amazon rain forest. I thought for a long while that these subjects interested him, and years would pass before I knew my father stole, snuck whatever spare books he could find into his trousers, as he carried the weight of all his past crimes.

He ended every reading with a section of the Quran, which he kept with him always. I followed his voice, imitating each tremble and pause. After he finished, he seated himself closer to the lantern and contorted his fingers into shadow animals.

The incense from my mother's puja room drifted toward us on the steps. Burnt lavender reminded me of her presence, of her prostrated in front of a pedestal of Hindu gods. A bronze Kali statue stood in the center with garlands, the goddess wide-eyed and furious. Hanging between my mother's collarbones on a gold chain was Lord Ganesh himself.

I was not allowed in the puja room for reasons I had yet to understand. Like all children, I vowed to disobey. The first time I crossed into the room, my mother was asleep, and I closed my eyes, covered my head in case the roof clawed open and Kali floated above me in the clouds, her tongue a hungry red serpent. I waited for the floor to shake, for the gods in their thrones to banish me, for my mother to wake and find me. Even now when I am late for work at the library and struggle with a pair of cotton stockings, I hear my mother's voice from the puja room, calling out to the heavens. *Shiva, what would you like to eat today? Lakshmi, should I dress you in an orange sari or a yellow sari?* She spoke to them as if they were her children.

I only saw my father enter the puja room once. He knelt down and left a red smear on the stone surface of the Shiva lingam. My mother must have noticed because she spoke that night directly to him during the evening meal.

"I think a thief visited us today," she said.

"Oh." My father nodded and put down his cup of water. He never drank tea or coffee, which to my mother was another grievance against him. He abstained for moral reasons, I supposed, a one-man boycott of the plantations he had toiled on for much of his childhood. Or perhaps the caffeine did not agree with his bowels.

Some mornings my father walked me to school after prayers.

He waited for me by a bullock cart on the side of the road, seated on a stump with his hand cupped under his chin as he admired the cattle. I dressed with care those days, ironed my school clothes, combed my hair until strands were scattered on the floor.

On seeing me, he would exclaim, "What a beautiful day," as cows defecated nearby.

He held my hand while we walked, the hot air pressed between us. In those crowded streets my father never loosened his grip. If we recognized someone, a neighbor or a peddler, my father regarded them distantly. His hand stiffened in one long, breathless pause.

His aloofness contained him in strange ways, forced him to seek companionship elsewhere, in books. When I held his hand, his shadow extended around me, protected me from the gaze of the sun and kept me in the dark. My loneliness spread from his fingertips. Eventually I shortened our walks, feigned tardiness and ran off before we reached the schoolyard, his sweat pooled in the base of my palm.

At school, we sat in rows according to name. I sat near the front by the window facing Mr. Chandra's garden that had glory lilies, blue poppies, and rare vegetables like apple gourd. My classmate Ashraf, who was the only other Muslim in my class, sat beside me for all my school days. He often looked out the window, and the schoolmaster would hover above him and say his name sharply in short syllables, and he would flinch from the proximity.

He performed poorly on exams. When we were all bent over, writing, he stared elsewhere for answers, at crows settling on branches, at thin clouds slowly disappearing.

His great-great-grandfather had moved from Tehran and had worked in the government, and the barest knowledge of his ancestry crowned Ashraf as an exile. With his nose raised, he spoke of Persia's superiority. "Tagore is no match for our Rumi," he pronounced, waving his arm with the declaration though he had never visited Iran. Both his parents were tailors.

I was envious then of his certainty, how surely he placed himself in history. Holding only a twig, he fleshed out descendants and ancestors until he beheld a tree, ripe with the past. Perhaps because he lived with his grandparents, spent time with his cousins down the street, it was easy to imagine what had come before.

On my twelfth birthday, my father brought me to the cinema. My mother accompanied us, dressed in a fancy sari trimmed with gold sequins, and I didn't remind her that we would be sitting in the dark. It was a film starring Tarun Kumar, one of my mother's many love interests. On seeing him on-screen, she turned to me and whispered, "It is a shame he is not like his older brother, Uttam Kumar," as if she knew them both intimately. During the scenes when the hero held the heroine close to his chest and said he loved her more than his life, loved her beyond the tallest mountain peak, my mother gripped my hand and even in the dark I could see the tears on her face.

After we returned home, my father and I took a walk. He asked me if I enjoyed the film, and I told him I did. He seemed satisfied and informed me of the ending of the latest book he was reading. Then, like he always did, he told me how it related to the Quran. Whenever I picked up the encyclopedia on birds, I thought of surah 67, verse 19: *Have they not seen the birds above them expanding their wings and drawing them in? None holds them except the Most Merciful. Surely He sees everything.*

We stopped at a water pipe, where two boys were filling up a metal pot, and my father parted his lips. Before he spoke, I asked him, "Why did you take Ma's family name?"

In the cabinet, I had discovered a photograph of my mother

as a schoolgirl. I recognized her immediately, her stubborn gaze and exacting features buoyed by her posture. Under her portrait was the name she was known by, Lakshmi Choudary. I cannot recall what my father called her, only how he addressed her through me. "Tell your mother we need more kerosene," or "Where is your mother?" He spoke of her as if she were separate from him, and he had not married her, taken her name, belonged to her.

At twelve, I had grown to my father's height, and when he turned toward me, I looked into his eyes, which reminded me of dark, wet pebbles, the hardness unlike him. I could stare at him for hours, and he would slip through my fingers, become no more than water in a teacup.

He placed his hand on my shoulder. "No," he said. "It is *my* name."

We had a radio, a black box covered on one side with circular mesh that was as thin as mosquito netting. Voices pressed against the screen, and I sat near and listened to distant sounds that felt close, drifting in like an evening breeze. My father had built the radio, recovered materials for a circuit board over the span of a year. It was not extraordinary then because he was my father and expectations for one's father are persistently growing when one is young. Only later did I understand his unnatural aptitude, how years of picking leaves did not prepare him for labor as a mechanic and that building a radio was both remarkable and inconsequential.

We listened to songs late into the night, the volume low while my mother slept. The sound murmured around us like crickets, and I imagined a diminutive orchestra of flute, veena, and tabla players hidden underneath a leaf.

For an hour at night, a woman announced news headlines. They never seemed to concern me. Problems with the dam in Mettur and the poor jute production in Orissa because of drought were no different from the mention of foreign nations. My father smoked a beedi while he listened. The ceremonial act reminded me of my mother lighting incense in the puja room, her gods floating through ribbons of smoke.

He propped his back against the wall and with an arm folded behind his head, he stared up, past the roof, past the Calcutta skyline, and waited for some far-off news. When the Bangladeshi War broke out in 1971, he arrived home one March evening with his hands bloody with ink. He did not shower but stayed by the radio smoking beedi after beedi, the white tip smudged black. Sweat stains darkened his shirt. If my father drank, he would have been a diligent alcoholic, slugging each bottle of toddy until it was clean and empty.

Listening to the news reports of war, my father looked remorseful and unkempt. Hair circled his face in wild, prickly rays, and dust from the street colored his skin in a sickly hue. He had not been praying, and during this lapse I prayed twice as hard for both of us. He slept by the radio as a woman's voice announced a fraction of the dead for the day—a university professor, an eight-year-old schoolboy, a pregnant woman—and my father closed his eyes as if the woman had called his name too.

The company of those familiar, unknown voices soothed me as a child even if they filled me with nightmares. I was more fearful of silence. Even now, when I return home from work, I turn on the television to some channel and listen to news about car crashes, murders as I complete my nightly routine.

Sometimes at work I skim one of the letters my mother sent me. She often describes my father's preference for reading over talking, and when I turn to the clock, suddenly the orderliness of my days falls to pieces, and my father sits in the Devonfield library with a book. I picture him underlining words with his fingers, returning again and again to some passage, his hands spread out on the page, and I stand weeping over a patron's library book, stamping the due date, telling her to take care as I close the empty library in the winter darkness. And she holds the door to ask, "What's wrong? Why do you cry?"

The year I turned fifteen, Ashraf, the other Muslim in my classes, visited our house frequently. My mother believed nothing fit her properly, her proportions as unpredictable as her temperament. She sent her clothing to Mr. Sanjay, a tailor she trusted, for alterations but on receiving her clothing she seemed disappointed, and spent hours examining seams, checking to see if threaded lines ran straight or crooked.

After my mother believed a blouse Mr. Sanjay stitched was too tight, she began consulting Ashraf's parents. His father visited the house and scrawled numbers on a sheet of paper, and in less than a week's time, Ashraf appeared at our doorway with my mother's belongings wrapped with a single string.

He left his sandals near the door and came inside to drink tea and eat sweets. Dressed in regular clothing, he sat on our floor and spoke of his knowledge of fabrics. He once rubbed the collar of my salwar, pinched the cloth with two fingers to describe the texture of the material. His thumb brushed against my skin.

The intimacy in the house did not extend to school, where I would remark on his nicely starched shirt, and he would say nothing, his eyes reaching for the window. I wondered how he withstood my mother's banter, the repetitions in her speech that made her seem more forgetful than she really was, but Ashraf was infatuated with my mother. One evening while I was studying for my final examination in mathematics, Ashraf visited my mother simply for a cup of tea. They sat together on the floor, and Ashraf presented different patterns for blouses. "This is the latest fashion," he said and revealed a square of cloth with purple mango designs. He described the cut and my mother listened attentively. He stared at her fair skin and green eyes as though appraising some rare textile. Before he left I caught him looking between my mother and me, a smile on his lips.

My father encouraged Ashraf's presence and hoped, perhaps, we would marry. "He's a good Muslim boy," he announced on more than one occasion, and later, when there was no longer any chance of a proposal, I learned how he had set aside his favorite books for me to take as bridal gifts. I never told my father about my feelings for Ashraf, but he must have known, my awkwardness more telling than any proclamation I could have made.

After our yearly examinations, my mother invited him over and served us sweets in celebration, and instead of picking a buttery laddoo he stood up and kissed my mother on the lips so naturally she didn't react. She walked away to the kitchen and asked if we wanted tea. The next day when Ashraf's father came for measurements, my mother was silent, said nothing of the incident, but I saw her eyes, wide with what I thought was guilt.

Even after the kiss, I still assumed our age guaranteed the promise of our union, that his affection for my mother was pure fancy and in time he would come to his senses. After my father returned home, I waited for Ashraf, became insolent when he did not show, and when he did, I was quiet, moved around the house, sullen and irritable, to show his presence did not affect me, brought me no joy. I followed him with my eyes, noticed the sores along patches of stubble, and thought he might have begun to shave but had given up. He had a circular birthmark near his mouth that disappeared when he smiled. And his nose, an unlikely arc, looked so much straighter from the front that to see him, to really see him, I had to be at all angles at once, suspended above him like the gods, like smoke.

When I sat to do work, my mother dug her hands into my

hair and combed the long strands with her fingers and braided them. The simple, unexpected act felt loving, my mother's fingers scratching at my scalp, but perhaps she was searching for the secret to the thickness. She could not understand how I lost so much from my ruthless brushing and still had hair to spare, unlike her with her hair cut to her shoulders because of thinness. "You will regret when it's gone," she would say.

I had vague notions of beauty, thought somehow that its properties did not affect me, but by looking at Ashraf, I began to see myself more clearly and would catch my face in a passing mirror, in the reflective glass of storefronts, in a pot of water, the light glancing on the surface. Many days I was startled by my image, at the roughness of my features, the way everything appeared unfinished.

One afternoon, when my mother slept outside in the back, Ashraf delivered a blouse. He decided to explore the house and walked freely with his sandals on. He opened each drawer of my mother's cabinet and left the last drawer slightly ajar so that the matchbooks and undergarments peeked out. He shook the radio to hear what was inside. My father's books fascinated him. He flipped through them, not minding the words or the drawings. "Your father, he read all this?" he asked. In the puja room, he touched each god, rubbed his thumb along Lord Ganesha's trunk. I did not stop him, and for days I wept, unable to look at anything except the sky.

After he finished with the puja room, he counted my fingers, one to eleven, and I thought of the days I had spent arguing whether he cared for me. "Strange, isn't your father," Ashraf said, "not belonging anywhere. Like you."

PICKING UP THE silver pieces of a hand mirror one Sunday morning, my father showed me the marks on his calf from a snakebite. "It happened so long ago," he said. "It looks like someone else's leg." I don't know why he showed me that past injury, perhaps to demonstrate how something painful could eventually soothe. He gripped my right hand and cracked the knuckles of all six fingers, and the pain and relief spread into my bones, felt indistinguishable from each other.

I do not remember when I stopped relying on my father, but it must have been when I first noticed that he was old, that his body had aged too quickly for his years. From the rear, one could mistake him for a young boy, his gray hairs discreetly hidden. I too must have aged him. The nights I came home late as he waited by the radio, pretending to sleep, listening not for the music but for my footsteps.

I smoked beedis like he did, chewed paan until my teeth were all red, and when I arrived home, he spoke to me in his calm, steady voice and said nothing of it. He never punished me, as though he was afraid to inflict harm. Instead, he must have prayed for me, lowered himself onto his prayer mat and kissed the ground as he did my forehead before I slept.

During the summer months, the heat was unbearable in the day. It squeezed into my lungs, made me nauseous. I sat in a lonely corner of the house that was far from the window and kept quiet. But no matter how still I sat, how low I hushed my voice, I was burning up and the house with its three rooms and bowed roof could not hold me. I longed for the remote places in my father's books, the cold of the Arctic, the "blissful freeze" Larry Mathews described in his travels to see the aurora borealis. When the electricity was cut, I ran out into the night, wandered.

When I was between the ages of sixteen and eighteen, my mother became more concerned with me, mostly my body, with how it was changing. She was impressed by the tightness of her blouses on me. The fat on my arms tore through her narrow sleeves and the swell of my hips made a grandmother passing us on her way to the temple remark, "You will have many children." Some days I caught my mother staring at me in the same manner she appraised strangers. She would tense and look away.

I stopped schooling after the eleventh standard. My schoolwork did not interest me, and though my father protested for what seemed like the first time, I did not budge and he relented. He found me work at a nearby all-girls college, working in the canteen. I think he hoped the proximity of scholars and students would make me reconsider, but he could not afford the schooling, and I had not earned the marks for a government scholarship.

Before partition, the college was named after Begum Roquia Sakhawat Hussain, the woman who wrote *Sultana's Dream*. It was the first book I read in English by myself. I understood little about the utopia she described, where women ruled the world and men were hidden, secluded. The fact that Roquia wrote in English appealed to me more than the content. I asked my father countless times, "Who translated it from Bengali?" "No one." And I continued to argue. "How could she write in English? It was published in 1905."

In hopes to continue my learning, my father presented me with books to read. I opened them after the lunch crowd departed and sat cross-legged next to the freezer, which I discovered—after asking my Hindu manager, "Which way is west?"—revealed the direction of Mecca when the ice melted on the floor during power outages. In between the pages were fresh leaves, and I pictured my father walking, picking young leaves from the lowest branches, his head raised instead of lowered as it once had been when he drifted over tea bushes on the hills of Ceylon.

At work, I dealt with meat. The rest of the workers were Hindu and professed vegetarians and could not handle raw meat, but I suspect if I were not there, they would have completed the task without complaint. My mother disapproved of my occupation, said I deserved better, and grieved I believe more for herself than for me.

My father was different. To disappoint him was an acknowledgment of a deep failing. Only years later, with my mother imploring me to see him, when I was living with a man twice my age, did I understand his regret as fear of the murder he committed, fear that I would not forgive him.

I met Rahul because of my father. I was looking over his encyclopedia of birds in the park when Rahul sat beside me.

"What is that one?" he said and pointed to a crow.

I stared at him. He wore a charcoal suit in the hottest month of the year. He was sweating and dabbed his head with a beige handkerchief that looked stained.

"That is a rare bird."

He nodded and kept looking from the bird to me.

"You only find it on earth," I continued.

He didn't laugh, and his calm face moved in me such laughter that I needed to hold on to the bench. He later admitted how nervous he was chatting with me. He had not talked to a woman since his wife's passing. I would discover he had mistaken me for someone older, but at that point it would not matter.

He was a mathematics professor at the university. He had noticed me on campus many times, always with a book. He was an eccentric sort of man, who was fond of speaking to himself and rolling up his pant legs to his knees when he walked around the school. I was intrigued by him.

He was childish in the way he insisted on counting certain patterns on the wall or stretching his arms four times from side to side before he stood up. When I read to him, he closed his eyes. The first time he did this I slammed the book so hard against the table that he gasped and stared at me, bewildered of his crime. In the beginning, I thought these habits were linked to his mathematical mind. Though he did not believe in God, the behavior seemed ritualistic, measured with certainty.

"I believe in Einstein," he told me one day, and when I said nothing, he squeezed my hand, the right one. "I believe in people."

My mother was cordial when she met Rahul. She did not take him into her arms or kiss his cheeks as she would a proper son-in-law. She treated him as a dignitary, with a respectful aloofness. She did not mention the circle of baldness or the way his chin rippled into pouches. Throughout the evening she gazed at Rahul's head and then at my father's crown of black and silver hair.

Rahul did not seem uncomfortable seated on the floor in our house but my father did. He held on to his chin and looked down.

"You like teaching?" my father asked.

"Very much."

Rahul was older than my father by three years. Looking at them, they might have been friends, old classmates, if not for the circumstances. My father said little to him, never lifted his hand as Rahul spoke of his new job and all our preparations for our move to London.

My mother looked out the window. "London is far."

"It's a very posh place. There will be people from all over the world." Rahul paused. "They even have good Bengali food."

My mother nodded. She didn't believe him.

"My grandfather was part of the British infantry in the Great War," my mother said. "He lost an arm to the cold. It froze."

I thought my mother selfish then. That she spoke so unkindly of my hopes.

At dusk my father stood up for prayer. He looked over at me, and I avoided his eyes. I did not follow him. When I traveled across the ocean to a cold London street, I held a handful of snow until my fingers went numb.

In the library, there is a painting of two parentheses on a white canvas like the dark curve of hands holding an invisible ball. Clarissa, my coworker, told me it is modern art. When I asked what it meant, she explained that the art is considered abstract, very difficult to understand.

Clarissa is a plump woman with a freckled, jovial face and a strong cockney accent. She grew up in the East End, a few streets over from Brick Lane, so on our first encounter she greeted me with *Assalam Alaikum.* I mirrored her and then responded in Bengali, and she waved her arms and said, "That's all I know."

She works with me at the desk in the children's section, which includes young adults and is, according to Clarissa, a tricky age group. She recently organized a reading for *Bloody Days of Girlhood* over the disapproval of some of the parents. After I calmed an angry mother, Clarissa placed her hand on my arm and the band of her pink pearl wedding ring dug into my skin. "Thank the Lord for you Bengalis."

Whenever I have spare time, I walk around the library and pause at the painting, take a seat at one of the empty tables. Other than a trip to a gallery in London, I have not viewed much art. Last Thursday, when my favorite patron visited, a child named Kareem, I asked him what he thought of the painting, and he dragged a chair to the wall and stood on the striped cushion. "It's like an outline of the world," he said, "without borders." He pressed his face into the empty space. "I'm a country."

When one of the older librarians passed, I asked Kareem to step off the chair. He jumped and did a quick bow before smiling with the same toothy smirk as the chipmunks on his T-shirt. He ran off into the stacks, stealing glances back at me as I stood in my dress and woolen jacket, my arms crossed over my chest. There are days I imagine that Kareem is my son. That my husband is still well, and I wait not for the pain that will seize his heart but for laughter, a strong morning wind.

My mother calls me during emergencies or holidays, and with all her excuses for the call, I know she wants to feel my voice. Often when my mother writes to me, she mentions my father's strange customs, the way he stares at birds and greets people by rubbing his ear. And I think of my father looking up into my face, belonging nowhere, living within his skin like an undiscovered nation. In her most recent letter, my mother mentions my father's passing, and I read the letter again and again. My mother's handwriting is sloppy, unlike her.

I rub my thumb against the ink until the paper creases, loses shape. I think of the week the letter has traveled to my doorstep, and how my mother did not call, how she could not bear to hear my voice or let me hear hers. It is signed *with love.*

A NOTE ABOUT THE AUTHOR

Akil Kumarasamy is a writer from New Jersey. Her fiction has appeared in *Harper's Magazine*, *American Short Fiction*, *Boston Review*, and elsewhere. She received an MFA from the University of Michigan and has been a fiction fellow at the Fine Arts Work Center in Provincetown and at the University of East Anglia. *Half Gods* is her first book.